what's a Girl to do?

JANET L. FOLGER

Multnomah Publishers® *Sisters, Oregon*

Some names, locations, and identifying details
have been changed to protect the identity of individuals.

WHAT'S A GIRL TO DO?
published by Multnomah Publishers, Inc.
Published in association with Loyal Arts Literary Agency, LoyalArts.com
© 2004 by Janet L. Folger
International Standard Book Number: 1-59052-330-X

Cover design by Kevin Keller/Design Concepts
Cover image by Laureen March/Corbis
Interior design/typeset by Katherine Lloyd, The DESK, Bend, Oregon

Italics in Scripture are the author's emphasis.
Unless otherwise indicated, Scripture quotations are from:
The Holy Bible, New International Version © 1973, 1984 by International Bible Society,
used by permission of Zondervan Publishing House

Other Scripture quotations are from:
The Holy Bible, New King James Version (NKJV) © 1984 by Thomas Nelson, Inc.
New American Standard Bible® (NASB) © 1960, 1977, 1995 by the Lockman Foundation.
Used by permission.
Holy Bible, New Living Translation (NLT) © 1996.
Used by permission of Tyndale House Publishers, Inc.
All rights reserved.
The Holy Bible, King James Version (KJV)

Multnomah is a trademark of Multnomah Publishers, Inc.,
and is registered in the U.S. Patent and Trademark Office.
The colophon is a trademark of Multnomah Publishers, Inc.

Printed in the United States of America

For information:
MULTNOMAH PUBLISHERS, INC.
POST OFFICE BOX 1720 • SISTERS, OREGON 97759

Library of Congress Cataloging-in-Publication Data
Folger, Janet L.
    What's a girl to do? / by Janet L. Folger.
        p. cm.
Includes bibliographical referencces.
    ISBN 1-59052-330-X (pbk.)
    1. Single women--Religious life. I. Title.
    BV4596.S5F65 2004
    248.8'432--dc22
                                                                    2003021598

04 05 06 07 08 09 10—10 9 8 7 6 5 4 3 2 1

To single people—the most untapped group of world changers.
God has a mission for you right now:
Follow Him and He will take care of everything else.

So do not throw away your confidence; it will be richly rewarded.
You need to persevere so that when you have done the will of God,
you will receive what he has promised.

HEBREWS 10:35–36

Contents

Special Thanks

This book is also dedicated to my mom, Beth E. Folger, my pep-talking confidante, who has listened to more hours of boyfriend woes than anyone else. Mom, you are the greatest encourager I have ever met, heard of, or read about. Your enthusiastic support surpasses that of Jacobs field—with the Indians in the World Series. Thank you for being such a godly adviser and my most consistent and dedicated prayer warrior. I am so grateful that God blessed me with such an incredible, joyful, generous, positive, uplifting, fun, creative, and godly mother. But beyond all those things, in the same person, He has given me my best friend. Thank you for all that you've done and all that you are. I hope to be like you one day.

Thanks also to my dad, James B. Folger, who would hand the phone to my mom when I stopped talking about world issues (and what's wrong with the car) and started talking about guys. Dad, your counsel about not listening to everyone else—since I'm the one who will have to live with the results—was good. I should have heeded it a lot more. Your quick wit and uncommon sense helped guide and direct me, keeping me moving forward. And I have to believe that the advice you gave to the guys I dated—like how they "needed a haircut" or should "consider getting a job" or "purchasing a watch" (to prevent late-night calls)—could only help steer them on the right path as well. Thanks for always being there with practical help and unwavering love and support, for coming to every speech, and for giving my books away to strangers in the bank and grocery store. I'm not sure what it meant to the people on the street, but it has meant the world to me.

A Special Thank-You to My Prayer Warriors:

Your continued intercession on my behalf has paved the way for everything God has done (and will do) in my life. It is the greatest gift you could ever give me...and after reading this book, I know you'll have the motivation to step things up! My life is different because of you, and I cannot begin to thank you enough: the Faith2Action Prayer Force; Korie Kapal, the K-pal God sent me to make up for all my "toxic friends"; Greg and Karen Darby and the Christian Interactive Network—living, breathing, answered prayer; Vic Elliason, Gordon, Karen, Jim, and the VCY radio network; Wanda Sanchez, radio producer and friend; Todd, Tanya, Justin, and Emily Folger—the Folger family prayer team; Aunt Sue Folger, whose prayers started me in Christian radio while in college; Matt Jacobson; Fred Hammack; Mickey Carauna, my airport buddy and praying friend; Andy Piccolo, who better start praying for me now that he's listed; Betty McGuire, my Minnesota prayer warrior; Payton Slagle; Margie Moriarty from Columbus, Ohio; Jim Carter; Bill and Nancy Doran; Bill and Betty Runde; John Herald—

researcher extraordinaire; Ross Conley of F2A newsletter fame; Philip and Bianca Nerenberg, who volunteer full-time to book my trips; all the kids at Alphabet Acres Christian Daycare; Lisa and A. J. Velazquez; Aunt Lynne and Uncle Jim Mackle; Debbie Payton; Carol and Don Van Curler, my Michigan "parents" (who gave out as many copies of my books as my real parents!); Louie and Marilyn Feiber; Lil Onstad, my Florida "mom"; Uri Katz; Abby Welch; Nathan Welch; Julie Stickler; Kathleen McGervey; Deirdre O'Sullivan; Marty Angell, Matthew Albert Giambrone, Karen Purre, Debbie Coker, Rachel Keller, Lisa Frechette, Karla Gushue, Bud and Marie Skedel; Allison and Romeo DeMarco; Janet Vigilante; Gail Coniglio; Bill and Diane Shott; Cheryl and Jim Krickhan; Sharon Best; Marlene Rice; Maxine Makas; Nancy Britt; Guyla Mills, who has been praying for me since I met her in Nebraska four years ago; Molly Grigg, who fasted for me after meeting me at a breakfast in Tampa; Debbie Christenson; Sharon Blakeney (sending up prayers from Texas); Dottie Wobb; Brother Lou Nordone; my San Diego "sisters" Mary Hammack, Pricilla Schreiber, and Patty Casares; Carol Hansen; Andrea Yorke; my Ohio Right to Life prayer warriors, Lorraine Schmidt and Judy Gregory; John and Petra Jakubczyk; Madeline Jakubczyk, the lady whom God woke up and told to pray for me in Evansville, Indiana; and the School of Prophets: Sarah, Lynda, Mary, Victoria, Melva, Aida, Samuel, Sharon, Catherine, Sharon B., and Daisy. And to others too many to name, who are so godly that they will keep praying for me even though they're not mentioned.

You've Got to Be *Kidding!*

S o my publisher said he wanted me to write a book.

Great! Something on one of the cultural issues we'd talked about? The Bible study I'd made a start on?

No, he said he wanted me to write a book on being single.

My response? "You've got to be *kidding!*" There are plenty of books on relationships. *Kissing Dating Goodbye. Kissing Dating Hello. Lady Not Dating. I'm So Happy Being Single that I Think I'll Write a Book about It.*

Blah, blah, blah.

As you may have guessed, I'm not into books like that. No doubt they make for good reading—though my friend Andy might disagree. He asked a girl to meet him at a bookstore for their first date, and while she was waiting she bought *I Kissed Dating Goodbye.* He never saw her again.

No kidding.

Maybe next time he'll show up on time.

Writing a book about dating just isn't my thing. Not my area of expertise. When I told my friend Kathleen, she couldn't stop laughing. Not a real vote of confidence.

But then I started thinking about it. Maybe I *have* learned some things. Maybe I could add something useful to the mix that hasn't been said already. So I e-mailed my publisher to say I would consider it.

Then I broke up with my boyfriend.

When my publisher telephoned to ask why I hadn't responded to his subsequent e-mails, the call went something like this: "You can forget about the book. I can't even write a *pamphlet*. How in the world am I supposed to give advice when I can't handle my own love life?"

You may be tempted to stop reading now. That's okay (as long as you've already bought the book!). But wait a second.

In his pep talk, my publisher told me that the thing I have going for me is honesty. Not that everyone else out there is lying, but sometimes you wonder if they're telling the whole truth. You know, the things you really feel, things that seldom make it into print—the kind of stuff you would tell your friends over coffee.

He told me to picture myself in a coffee shop, catching up with friends, trading stories, binding each other's wounds, laughing, refocusing, and reemerging as the women God wants us to be.

So I did.

one

The Coffee Shop

Welcome to Folger's Coffee Shop. We'll be ordering something chocolate with whatever we're drinking. Maybe a brownie with hot chocolate. Desperate times call for desperate measures.

So, I'm going to talk to you as if you're one of my inner circle of friends hanging out with me at the coffee shop. I'm going to tell you what I'd tell them—like the fact that we don't always see things from God's perspective. We may *know* that men are human beings made in God's image, but sometimes it's hard to see them that way. At one point directly following the breakup, I suggested the working title *Women Are from Venus; Men Are...Jerks*. It didn't fly.

I remember being the speaker at a women's conference when I really didn't feel like speaking. I had just gone through a heart-wrenching breakup. Not just any breakup, mind you. It was *the* breakup—the one where the wedding date was already set. Maybe you know what I'm talking about—the one where you pored over books of castlelike bed-and-breakfasts in Italy to pick out where you're going to spend your honeymoon. Yeah, *that* one. Well, we broke up and it was brutal. I didn't feel very spiritual. Couldn't fake it. Couldn't put on a plastic smile and pretend, "Everything's great! Praaaaise God! I'm soooo blessed!" *Pass the saccharine.*

I tried to overcome what I was feeling in order to make it through the speech but didn't quite manage it. So I told the audience that earlier in the day I had used my ex-boyfriend's shirt to clean out the crud in my refrigerator. The scary thing is I wasn't kidding. About half of them laughed. The other half looked sort of frightened. But I'm convinced that all of them could relate.

Waiting on God

Here's what I know: God has a mission for you. Yes, *you*. He has an assignment—a plan of action—for you *right now*. He wants you off of the sidelines and into the game.

But Satan doesn't. It's that simple. We're in this spiritual war, and Satan will use anything he can to keep us from God's perfect plan. He'll hit us when we're down: "For our struggle is not against flesh and blood, but against the rulers, against the authorities, against the powers of this dark world and against the spiritual forces of evil in the heavenly realms" (Ephesians 6:12).

And although Satan knows that God has everything under control, with an exciting and perfect plan for your life—with perfect timing (believe it or not)—he's gonna tell you otherwise. Satan's a liar, after all—that's what he does. And I believe that his favorite targets are those who could very well be the most effective members of God's kingdom: single people.

Satan is going to tell you that while God is taking care of everyone else—including all your friends who are getting married—He has somehow forgotten about you.

It's a lie.

You're alone now—like me—because God has something He wants you to do. Something so critically important to His mission that Satan has to come up with a way to stop it.

Make no mistake: Satan will pull out every stop to prevent what he knows you could do for the kingdom of God. I'm talking about the big guns here—the rocket launchers designed to debilitate even the most faithful soldiers in God's army:

* "You're all alone...."
* "God has forgotten you...."
* "He has abandoned you...."
* "You're a failure...."
* "A loser..."
* "Nobody wants you...and maybe nobody ever will...."
* "Look around you—everyone else is happy except for you...."

* "See those babies? Cute, huh? Take a good look, because you'll probably never have any."

Does any of that sound familiar?

Pretty harsh stuff, but remember—this is war. All's fair in love and war—and this one is *both*. If you couldn't be used so mightily, Satan wouldn't have to go after you so fiercely. The trouble is, when you're under attack, all those lies sound *true*—absolutely convincing and seemingly irrefutable.

How do I know? Because I've believed them too. Just like you. Just like all single people out there—whether in their twenties, thirties, forties, or beyond. Whether they have dates coming out of their ears, have been proposed to seventeen times, or haven't been on a date in years. Ask around and see if I'm right. Satan is an equal opportunity destroyer. (He's got a different set of weapons for our married friends, but that's another book entirely.)

You know, it's not about being married. It's about being married to the *right* person. Because marriage to the wrong person is worse than anything we face as singles. I'm pretty sure our divorced readers could verify that divorce is far more painful than waiting ever was.

But I don't just hate waiting. I *despise* it.

In fact, I never once prayed for patience because I know how you get it—God makes you wait and wait and wait (and wait) for the answer. Not my thing. If I had to name a flower that most characterizes me, it would be "impatiens."

But the only thing worse than waiting on God is *wishing* you had waited on Him.

The good news is, you don't have to sit around waiting. When we obey God rather than believing the lies, not only will He use us mightily; He will also take away the misery of waiting. It's the difference between sitting on the bench watching the clock and actually playing in the game. There's no doubt which goes by faster. While we're waiting for God to send along Mr. Right, we need to get in the game of life.

LED AWAY TO LIFE

Single, cute, and lonely. That was Linda, who volunteered at Ohio Right to Life while I was legislative director there. There wasn't anyone for her to meet in the office, but she came faithfully, once a week, to stuff envelopes. Sometimes she even got to run them through the postage machine. Exciting stuff, huh? She wanted to obey God's command: "Rescue those being led away to death" (Proverbs 24:11).

We became friends and had a lot of fun together. Things weren't going so well for Linda. But things seemed to be going great for me. I ended up dating two of her friends. And though I didn't know it at the time, she had a huge crush on one of them.

Much later, Linda told me about her "special night" with Bill. She had invited him over to her house for dinner. Things were going well, when he cozied up to her and said, "Would it be okay if I asked you a...personal question?"

"Yesssss?" She was convinced this was "it." He was finally going to ask her how she felt about him, or if she would go out with him on a real date.

"Do you think your friend Janet would go out with me?"

Ouch.

This is where I have to tell you, my close friend at the coffee shop, that I wasn't a very good friend here. To be honest, I didn't mind Bill's interest. We dated for a short while—without mentioning it to Linda. If I could go back, I wouldn't have dated him, but at the time I had it all rationalized. Bill assured me that my feelings of reservation and guilt were unwarranted. He lobbied like a true professional. "Look, it's not like Linda and I ever went out," he reasoned. "So why shouldn't I be able to date someone I *want* to date just because you happen to know someone I don't want to date?"

Yeah, why should he be denied the privilege? He made a convincing case at the time—because I wanted to go out with him.

Then Linda introduced me to Tom—with the emphasis on how, unlike Bill, he was a *Protestant,* like me. I dated him too...for seven years.

Now imagine you're Linda and you have a crummy friend like me. While she's sitting at home, I have dates coming out of my ears. On the surface you'd probably say, "I'd rather be in Janet's situation." Right?

Things aren't always as they appear.

Don't get me wrong. I was having a blast. But what would you rather have? A blast dating guys who aren't your husband—or a few months without any dates until you meet your husband?

Linda couldn't see what God had for her just around the corner. But God knew.

This is where I redeem myself as a friend. Linda announced that she was moving across the state, and I threw her one of my best parties ever. I know, I know, it doesn't make up for dating the guy she liked, but keep reading—it gets better. I posted flyers with her picture everywhere—and everyone came to the volleyball cookout bash in her honor. Everyone. Including an obnoxious guy from New Jersey I had gone out with (I'll tell you about him later). I'm now convinced that I endured going out with him just so he could bring his friend—Linda's future husband—to my party. They met, fell in love, and are now married with five kids.

You wouldn't think a going-away party would provide an opportunity to meet someone—after all, Linda was moving across the state. But God knew. God can do anything. He could have put the guy in line behind her in the bank. All I know is that she was obedient to God's command to help stop the shedding of innocent blood, and because of her obedience she ended up meeting her husband.

Me? Well, after dating me, Bill became a priest. Before he was ordained, he came to a party of mine and told my other guests about how I had made him a "wonderful candlelight dinner—Cheerios." That probably helped drive him into the priesthood. Tom, the one I dated off and on (mostly off) for seven years, is now married. And the guy from New Jersey? I assume back in New Jersey.

That was almost ten years ago. And if I could choose, I'd pick Linda's situation over mine—even with all the fun times I had.

I would rather be alone for a few months, and then meet my husband, than date for years without finding him.

When you feel like Linda did—alone and no apparent prospects on the horizon—remember that things are not always as they appear. Be obedient in what you do know—even if it's just stuffing envelopes—because God will bless you in ways you can't see, think of, or imagine.

Here's the bottom line: There is a God who intersected time and history to be nailed to a cross to pay your admission to heaven. That's how much He loves you. That's how much He wants to be with you. Regardless of where you are, regardless of what you feel or think, He is *for* you. And His plan for your life is best. Even when you feel differently. The good news is that our thoughts and feelings don't change the truth: God is *for* us.

And despite all the lies Satan has been throwing your way, the truth is that you're *not* alone. Jesus said He would never leave you or forsake you (Hebrews 13:5). Regardless of how you feel about what you see when you look in the mirror, you are created in the image of God. You have value, purpose, and meaning beyond words.

God has you where you are right now for a reason. You have an assignment from Him. And you may never again have the opportunity to fulfill that assignment the way you can right *now*—single, free from all the responsibilities that come with marriage and children. God wants you off the sidelines and in the game. But to be a player, you have to get your mind off what you *don't* have and start looking to Him and what He has for you!

If you trust God despite your circumstances and despite your feelings, you will be used by Him in ways you never thought possible. And, yes, when you're not standing around watching the clock, misery will be replaced with enormous productivity. This time in the "desert" will, at the very least, seem to go more quickly, allowing God's perfect plan for the right someone in your life to unfold more rapidly.

Listen, life is but a breath. It's so very short that if we really thought about it, it would bum us all out. We don't have a lot of time—certainly not enough time to sit around sulking about how things aren't going as we planned. Do you really think your life should be "on hold" until you have someone "to hold"?

If God has a mission for us, then I want in on it. I'm tired of waiting. I want to fulfill His plan for my life, and when my life doesn't seem to be what I would have designed for myself, it's all about trust. Dr. D. James Kennedy once said that all of life could be summarized with two words: "Trust God." That's true whether we're single, divorced, widowed, or married.

Trust God. His plan is better than anything we could dream up for ourselves. Don't believe me? Remember that guy in high school or college you were so crazy about—the one you thought you should marry? Realized differently, didn't you? When you wonder whether your plans might be better than what a loving, all-knowing God has for you, think about that. It might help.

The guy whose shirt I used to clean out my refrigerator? I'm thankful to God that I didn't marry him—now. God's plan, in retrospect, was best. By the way, I'm not advocating that you use the clothes of old boyfriends to scrub your appliances. I'm sure it's not what any of those other books would recommend. But I can tell you that I found it to be extremely therapeutic!

BATTLEGROUND OF THE MIND

It all starts in the mind—our thought life. This is the battleground, where it all happens. If we're not winning here, we're losing.

Satan comes to steal and destroy. Hitting people when they're down is his specialty. He wants to rob you of your happiness and your self-esteem. It's his job description. So don't be surprised when he tries to tell you that because some guy was a jerk, you are somehow to blame. Because some guy wasn't right for you, *you're* a loser. Then he'll to try to steal what God has for you next by getting you to focus on the past:

"Look at all the time you wasted."

"Look at how much of your life is gone."

"Look at all the things you'll never have."

This is where we have a choice: to believe the lies or to forcibly replace them with the truth. We'll talk more about this later, but it's so important I had to bring it up now. If you let them, those thoughts Satan keeps shooting into your mind can become so overwhelming that they'll keep you from concentrating on anything else. The Bible says, "And do not be conformed to this world, but be transformed by the renewing of your mind, that you may prove what is that good and acceptable and perfect will of God" (Romans 12:2, NKJV).

If you've let Satan control the stronghold of your mind, you may be having difficulty even reading this. If that's the case, stop and pray right now. Ask God to help you choose what is true. Jesus said, "Whatever you bind on earth will be bound in heaven, and whatever you loose on earth will be loosed in heaven" (Matthew 16:19). So bind Satan. Ask God to guard your mind and thoughts and to help you choose His thoughts the moment one of Satan's comes into your mind. Take every thought captive (2 Corinthians 10:5), and replace it with truth: "Finally, brothers [*uh, sisters*], whatever is true, whatever is noble, whatever is right, whatever is pure, whatever is lovely, whatever is admirable—if anything is excellent or praiseworthy—think about such things" (Philippians 4:8). Write them down in a journal—it will help.

Remember, this is *war.* And Satan has some tried-and-true buttons he pushes. If button A works with you, guess what? He's going to keep pushing it. If button B has a debilitating impact, that one will become his favorite. The bad news is, those thoughts are disguised as facts and logic. But once you know this, you can do something about it. You know the buttons Satan uses most often with you, and you know the results. Now recognize them as the lies that they are, and choose to feed your mind with the truth.

But let's not give Satan all the credit here—we do enough damage on our own. We have built up negative thinking habits. It's like backing out of a dirt driveway. No matter how you steer the car, the tires gravitate toward the well-worn ruts. Our brains tend to follow the same well-worn ruts: doubts, negative self-talk, unforgivingness. If this is what you've trained your brain to think, that's what you'll *continue* to think—unless you break out of the ruts and start driving a different way. When you feel your tires slipping into the ruts, turn your steering wheel sharply the other way and press on the gas. Start filling your mind with the truth of God, and the open road will be yours.

This is also true for the spoken word. Do *not* let yourself verbalize negativity. Not even in jest (that's one I have to work on). The Bible tells us of the power in the spoken word—there is life and death in the tongue (see James 3:3–10). God *spoke* the world into existence. He speaks of things that are not as if they are (Romans 4:17). What we speak reinforces what we believe and what we can expect to happen. Watch what you say—even to yourself. Replace the ruts of negativity with God's truth and you will start seeing Him bring that truth to pass.

We all go through the "guys are jerks" stage, so I know this is hard to imagine, but maybe, just maybe, he feels that *you* were the jerk. *Nah.* Well, it might be helpful here to say...at least *consider*...that perhaps we are not without fault. If every guy who breaks up with you tells you he doesn't like how critical and negative you are, maybe it's time to reevaluate. Maybe you *can* make some changes.

Maybe you've done more than make "mistakes"—maybe you've outright sinned. That's when you need to go to God, as David did: "Have mercy on me, O God, according to your unfailing love; according to your great compassion blot out my transgressions. Wash away all my iniquity and cleanse me from my sin" (Psalm 51:1–2). God will cleanse us if we humble ourselves, confess our sin, repent—that is, turn from it—and ask for His forgiveness. He'll blot out our sin and wash it away.

Don't beat yourself up over what is already done, because we know that God can work *all things* for our good (Romans 8:28). We can learn from past actions. We can prevent ourselves from going through this wilderness again—if we learn our lesson and take a different course the next time around.

ALL ABOUT EVAN

My friend Evan is usually the one who gets the calls from me from airplanes telling him how everything was going great and then just fell apart. A number of times he has said, "Jan, you should have called me. I could have told you it was coming."

"What do you mean?"

"Well, that's Satan's favorite button with you. Why *shouldn't* he keep using it if you keep letting it work for him?"

I met Evan when I went to Virginia Beach for an interview. Even though I didn't get the job, he became one of my best friends. I knew him as "Evan till Eleven," since that was when he got off work. He was my bellhop, and we hit it off right away. He carried my bags to the room and asked why I was in town. "A meeting," I told him.

He wouldn't let that go. "What kind of meeting?"

"Well, it's actually an interview."

"Who with?"

I couldn't think of any polite way to make this guy shut up, so I told him. "Pat Robertson and Ralph Reed." Ralph Reed was leaving Christian Coalition, and I had an interview for his job as executive director.

Hearing this, Evan gave me a special "Mustard Seed Pen" and

told me of the faith that moves mountains. Turns out he gives the pen to just about everyone he checks in.

Let me give you a glimpse of Evan. He went to Jerry Falwell's Liberty University on a tennis scholarship. A conservative Christian university, but Evan was…well…living on the edge. He told me about how he and his buddies "were witnessing to a Greek family one evening...how were we to know it was a *sorority* house?"

Well, not only were they not supposed to be there, they weren't allowed to be out after midnight. And the orange-parka-clad students on security detail were onto them. They saw Evan and his friends sneaking back on campus at 3:00 AM and started to chase them. But Evan's friends were jocks, and they all, narrowly, escaped.

To hear him tell it is a lot more fun. "Jan, we're running through the woods, but the 'Pumpkin Patrol' is right behind us— right? So we leap over the ditch—only not everyone makes it. We had to pull our buddies out of the mud, but the patrol was right on our trail. So we ducked behind buildings, crossed the railroad tracks, scaled a hill...and darted it to our buddy's dorm room unscathed. We barely made it just before the Pumpkin Patrol showed up—as we peeked out the windows, red lights were flashing everywhere. We high-fived each other like delinquent Olympians—although no one played our national anthem, we considered it a good night and went to bed. One of the resident assistants checked our room and found six guys covered in mud—stuff thrown everywhere. He just looked in, shook his head, and closed the door."

But Evan didn't let the story go untold. And word got around—all the way to the dean.

The dean called him into his office. "Evan, where were you on Friday night?"

Evan's version: "Jan, I totally lied. 'Well, my buddies and I went to see a late movie. The car broke down—gotta *hate* that—and so we had to walk all the way back.'" He was the smart-aleck kid who thought he was untouchable. You know the kind.

The dean just stared at him and said, "Evan—I *know* you're lying, but I can't prove it." Like this guy was a stereotype in a movie—*Ferris Bueller* comes to mind.

A short while later one of Evan's buddies got sent to the dean's office. His scholastic future must have been threatened, because under intense interrogation this guy spilled everything. Names, dates, and an outlined list of violations. Signed and notarized.

The next day Evan ran into the dean in the cafeteria. He slapped him on the back, and said, "Hey, Dean! How's it goin'?"

The dean was not amused. He pointed his finger in Evan's face and simply said, "My office. One hour."

So carefree Evan sauntered into the dean's office for a chat. The dean said, "Evan, remind me again what happened on that Friday we talked about."

And Evan poured it on again. "Late movie. Car broke down...gotta *hate* that..." The whole drill.

That was when the dean pulled out his legal pad and went through the itemized violations.

Evan's thinking, "Ouch. *That's* gonna leave a mark."

Turns out he had more than three times the reprimands needed to be kicked out of school.

The dean barked, "I want you and your friends off this campus in twenty-four hours—do you understand?"

It seemed pretty clear to Evan. He and his friends skipped mandatory chapel that night and went to the movies. Only this time their car really did break down. So they walked. Near the theater, Evan spotted Dr. Jerry Falwell pulling up to a Hardee's. He elbowed his buddy and said, "Watch this."

He went up to the car and knocked on the window. Dr. Falwell cranked it open about a quarter of an inch to see what he wanted.

This is where Evan turned on the charm. "Dr. Falwell, I just wanted to thank you for all you've done for the university...." He really meant it.

Before he could finish, Dr. Falwell said, "Hop in. What's your story, son?"

Evan eased into it. And Dr. Falwell told him, "You're just the kind of young man I want in my university."

"You don't understand, sir. It's too late for me. I've blown it, but I really appreciate the opportunity...and all you've done."

Dr. Falwell showed true Christian mercy. "No, *you* don't understand—I was young once too." It was his university, after all.

Evan glanced at his buddies and wondered if he could actually pull it off. "Well, I have these friends too...."

Dr. Falwell told him to write down their names. They were all going to get another chance.

I think it was the next day when Evan ran into the dean. "Hey,

Dean! I know I'm supposed to be gone, but I ran into a friend of yours—maybe you know him? Jerry Falwell?"

After that, Evan maintains, "I totally toed the line."

That's Evan. And though I never got kicked out of school, I can somehow relate to him. My friend Abby said, "The rules that apply to everyone else don't seem to apply to you."

"There might be some truth in that," I told her. "I think I'm illegally parked right now."

I'm trying to do better with that. I understand Evan is too.

I told you about Evan because it's the kind of story I'd share with friends in a coffee shop. But back to why I got started on it....

Remember, Satan is going to try to distract us from what God has for us. He'll push the buttons that work...and keep pushing them as long as they keep working. We create enough problems for ourselves, but toss a spiritual dimension into the mix and we don't stand much of a chance. When this happens—and it will happen—what are you going to do?

The only sure thing I know is that we must be grounded in God's Word. Get into the Word and start combating the lies so that when Satan pushes his tried-and-true button that says "God has forgotten about you. He doesn't care and won't answer your prayers," you will recognize it as a lie from the pit of hell and fill your mind with what you know to be true—God's words of hope, love, and encouragement.

God Is Good

* Who, then, is the man that fears the LORD? He will instruct him in the way chosen for him. He will spend his days in prosperity, and his descendants will inherit the land. (Psalm 25:12–13)

* Delight yourself in the LORD and he will give you the desires of your heart. Commit your way to the LORD; trust in him and he will do this: He will make your righteousness shine like the dawn, the justice of your cause like the noonday sun. (Psalm 37:4–6)

* Praise the LORD, O my soul; all my inmost being, praise his holy name. Praise the LORD, O my soul, and forget not all his benefits—who forgives all your sins and heals all your diseases, who redeems your life from the pit and crowns you with love and compassion, who satisfies your desires with good things so that your youth is renewed like the eagle's. (Psalm 103:1–5)

* Yet the LORD longs to be gracious to you; he rises to show you compassion. (Isaiah 30:18)

* "For I know the plans I have for you," declares the LORD, "plans to prosper you and not to harm you, plans to give you hope and a future." (Jeremiah 29:11)

* "The thief comes only to steal and kill and destroy; I have come that they may have life, and have it to the full." (John 10:10)

* And we know that God causes everything to work together for the good of those who love God and are called according to his purpose. (Romans 8:28, NLT)
* He who did not spare his own Son, but gave him up for us all—how will he not also, along with him, graciously give us all things? (Romans 8:32)
* Every good and perfect gift is from above, coming down from the Father of the heavenly lights, who does not change like shifting shadows. (James 1:17)

GOD'S SIDE OF THE STORY

Here's something else to focus on: God loves you. Maybe you've heard that statement so often that it seems kind of trite. Yes, God loves everyone, but what does that really mean? *How* does He love me? How can we really understand the love of a God we can't see? How can we feel the love of someone we can't even hold?

Beth Moore, in her Bible study *Breaking Free*, describes God's love in a way I've never heard before:

Psalm 127:3–5 says: "Sons are a heritage from the LORD, children a reward from Him. Like arrows in the hands of a warrior are sons born in one's youth. Blessed is the man whose quiver is full of them."

John 3:17 tells us God gave His Son for the salvation of people by sending Him into the world: God only had one arrow in His quiver. The most perfect arrow ever to exist. This arrow was a masterpiece, priceless to Him. Cherished far above all the hosts of heaven. Nothing could compare. His only heritage. His only Son. But as God looked on a lost world—desperate and needy and in the clutches of the enemy—His heart was overwhelmed. Though they had sinned miserably against Him and few sought Him, God had created them in love and could not love them less.

Love reached sacrificially into the quiver and pulled forth the solitary arrow. The quiver would now be empty, His cherished arrow in the hands of hateful men. Yes, God so loved the world; but God *also loved* His only begotten Son with inexpressible, divine affection. The divine dilemma: two loves. And one would demand the sacrifice of the other. Only one weapon could defeat the enemy of the soul—God's arrow. He positioned the weapon, pulled back the bow, steadied His grip, aimed straight for the heart. "And she brought forth her firstborn son, and wrapped him in swaddling clothes, and laid him in a manager" (Luke 2:7, KJV). God is FOR us. He has EARNED our trust.[1]

Just one more thing about God's love. We all know He sent His only Son because He loved the world, but let's take another glimpse at that. God created us and loved us and wanted to rescue us from our own sins, but if I were God, I would have called the whole thing off at this point:

They stripped him and put a scarlet robe on him, and then twisted together a crown of thorns and set it on his head. They put a staff in his right hand and knelt in front of him and mocked him. "Hail, king of the Jews!" they said. They spit on him, and took the staff and struck him on the head again and again. After they had mocked him, they took off the robe.... They led him away to crucify him.... Those who passed by hurled insults at him, shaking their heads and saying, "You who are going to destroy the temple and build it in three days, save yourself! Come down from the cross, if you are the Son of God!"... "Let God rescue him now if he wants him, for he said, 'I am the Son of God.'" (Matthew 27:28–31, 39–40, 43)

Imagine for a moment that you're God. You send your only Son to earth to save a sinful people, and they not only drive spikes into His hands and feet and leave Him hanging from them; they mock Him as they challenge Him to save Himself. That's where I would have canceled the whole salvation plan. Because you know what? These people didn't *deserve* to be saved. *Forget the whole thing.* I would have called in the legions of angels and showed them all— just before zapping their deplorable lives out of existence.

Good thing I'm not God. He loves us more than we can comprehend: He let His creation kill His Son—and stood by while they did it. That's *a lot* of love. "God demonstrates his own love for us in this: *While we were still sinners*, Christ died for us" (Romans 5:8).

Settle in your mind that God forever demonstrated His absolute love for you on the cross. That love will never change.

And God not only loves you; He is all-powerful, and that power is tapped through prayer. We need to spend a whole lot more time in prayer. When you go on your morning walk, or whenever is best for you, use the time to pray. Turn off the radio on your way to the office—you don't need to hear all those love songs right now anyway—and pray. Use your waiting time to pray—because prayer changes things.

We'll talk a lot more about prayer later on, but I couldn't wait for you to start doing something that will change your life. When you're standing in line at the grocery store or waiting for your dry cleaning—pray. Pray for God to intervene in your life right there. Pray for an opportunity to witness to someone in line.

Sometimes I carry a notebook in which I write down the verses that have meant the most to me. I focus on them in airline lounges when I'm waiting for my seating section to be called. I have quite a few entries from the time of the 2000 presidential election between George W. Bush and Al Gore, because I don't think I have ever prayed so hard for anything in all my life. I remember sitting on a plane with a book to read. But with the election results still in the balance, I didn't want to read it—it would take time away from praying, something that could determine the outcome.

Looking back, I know I made the right choice.

A SIMPLE YARD SIGN

God puts us in situations and environments to be a light for Him. You may be thinking, *It has to be something big.* But I've found that God also uses the small things we do. Simple things—like putting out a yard sign.

I put up a Bush-Cheney sign in my front yard during the 2000 presidential election. *Wow, huh?*

To me it was a simple act of obedience. Bush was pro-life and Gore was in favor of even partial-birth abortions. That's where they kill the child *during delivery* by sucking out its brain. I'm not kidding, and I'm not voting for anyone who could support that—Democrat or Republican. So I put up my yard sign.

Now, I live in a fairly liberal community—Broward County, Florida. You may remember hearing that name in the election recount coverage (that's how I spent *my* vacation!). I also live in a gated community, which is quite strict about what you can and can't do. I've gotten wrist-slapping notices for having rust splotches from the sprinklers on my fence. I've had tickets for a few blades of grass growing between the bricks in my driveway, for dead grass on the lawn, even for taking my garbage can out on the wrong day.

I was getting used to what I affectionately call the "Neighborhood Communist Association," but when they gave me a ticket for posting my Bush-Cheney sign, they had gone too far.

I remember coming home and seeing that my sign had been removed from my yard and placed at my door with one of their lovely notices. I thought, *I didn't realize that I signed away my First Amendment rights when I moved here.* Even more ridiculous was seeing every other house with a Gore-Lieberman sign—*untouched.* Apparently they were only enforcing their no sign regulation with Bush supporters.

So I put the sign back up in my yard.

And they took it down.

After another day of driving by about thirty untouched Gore signs, I put my sign back up.

This time they *took* my sign.

The Gore signs remained prominently displayed.

I was jogging around the neighborhood when I got an idea. People had all kinds of Halloween decorations hanging on their garages. Witches, ghosts, skeletons, pumpkins—they were all over the place. Okay, on the election-sign deal they had me on a technicality—yard signs were apparently illegal in this communist community—but there seemed to be no regulations against hanging things on your garage.

So I found the magnets some friends had used to decorate my house several months earlier (I'll tell you about this later)—a lot of big, round, heavy-duty magnets. And I spelled the word *BUSH* across my entire garage door in letters as big as me. Who needed a yard sign?

I left on a trip, and when I came back my neighbors had redesigned my BUSH magnets to read GORE.

Cute.

This was just after the election, so I spelled out the words BUSH WON.

I came back to the word BULL. (You remember how long the recounting went on?)

This was getting kind of fun. It was just after the certification by Secretary of State Katherine Harris, so I spelled out: BUSH WON 3 Xs.

Apparently they couldn't think of anything better than that, so they started stealing my magnets.

I had a huge banner from the recount rallies that said THOU SHALT NOT STEAL. So I hung that up for a while.

When I felt that I had made my point, I took it down. That's when people started coming out of the woodwork.

"*What happened?*"

"Have you given up the fight?"

"We were all counting on you!"

"Thank you for standing up to them!"

It seemed several people in the neighborhood—from a few streets over—were rooting for me in this little contest. I invited them all to my victory party, where over a hundred people came to celebrate the final outcome. My house was easy to find. It was the one with a *W* as big as the garage door on it. For George "W" Bush. With two spotlights on it.

We have to be a light wherever we are—and whatever our marital status, whatever the conditions. *Although a husband would've come in handy if someone had wanted to beat me up.* We only need to be obedient, and God will use us—even through something as simple as a yard sign.

Don't ever forget that we're in a spiritual battle.

You're probably saying to yourself, "I knew that." Well, you may know it, but you're going to forget. *I* forget all the time. I know you will too, because we're human, and we act on what we see and hear and feel. So we have to keep reminding ourselves.

God says that all the days ordained for me were written in His book before one of them came to be (Psalm 139:16). He has a plan—a mission for every one of us. He had it all spelled out before He ever formed you in your mother's womb. Did you hear that? You! You have a destiny. God put you on this earth at this precise point in history because He has something for you to do—right *now*.

Do you ever feel as though your life is like a movie? I do. Only it's not a movie. It's real. It's your *life*. You're starring in it, with God as the producer and director. He also wrote the script—after all, He is the Giver of life and the Author of our faith (John 6:33; Hebrews 12:2). That's where that omnipotence thing comes in handy. Yeah, being all knowing is definitely a plus if you're the one calling the shots. Now pair that with someone who loves you enough to *die for you*—that's who *I* want to take directions from. That's the kind of director you can trust to make whatever happens in the plot work for good—to lead your life story to a happily ever after.

This kind of exciting storyline isn't just for the "greats" in history. It's not only for biblical heroes. Because guess what? They were all ordinary people, just like you, and just like me. My ninety-four-year-old friend Greta knew Thomas Edison. Her father was his butler. She lived in one of his houses and got to meet all the people he entertained—people like Charles Lindbergh, Henry Ford, Calvin Coolidge, and the Colgates (yes, of toothpaste fame). All great men, but you know what? Greta tells me they were all just "ordinary people." Down-to-earth like everyone else.

Ordinary people can do incredible things. So can you. When you submit to God's plan for you—and let Him work through you—you can accomplish God-sized things that you could never accomplish on your own.

two

Does God Want You Married?

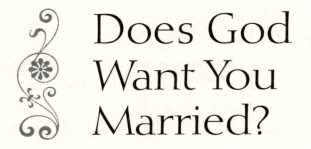

Many people never marry. We all know that. Some people don't *want* to. I'm fairly sure that's not you since you're reading this book. But what does God have to say? "Delight yourself in the LORD and he will give you the desires of your heart" (Psalm 37:4). I've been trying to delight myself in Him ever since. Want to know my prayer? *God, if the desires of my heart don't match Yours, then please change my desires.* I've prayed that and meant it. But as of today, I still want to be married. That gives me hope that God will fulfill that desire.

SHIPHRAH AND PUAH

I bought *The One Year Bible* because I wanted to try to read through the Bible again. I started last year and only made it to Exodus. Not something to brag about (though I did read many other parts). To increase my chances of making it through this time, I started reading on January 25, which is where Exodus begins in the one-year plan. Listen to what I found just this morning—something I never saw before—after Joseph died, Egypt had a bad king who hated the Israelites. He was afraid they were getting too numerous and wanted to kill them off. So he told the Hebrew midwives, Shiphrah and Puah (which I think is the Hebrew word for "I just bit into something *really* nasty"), to kill any male children birthed under their supervision.

Exodus 1:17 tells us what they did: "The midwives, however, feared God and did not do what the king of Egypt had told them to do; they let the boys live." When the king summoned them and asked why they had spared the boys, they said, "Hebrew women are not like Egyptian women; they are vigorous and give birth before the midwives arrive" (v. 19).

Okay, Pharaoh tells them to kill the baby boys, and they obey God rather than Pharaoh. Then they lie about it. Look what happens next: "So God was kind to the midwives and the people increased and became even more numerous. *And because the midwives feared God, he gave them families of their own*" (v. 20–21).

They feared God, they obeyed Him, and God gave them families of their own. If that's what God did for them, then I want to follow their lead. I'm really glad I'm working in the pro-life movement—at this moment in particular—to save babies from being killed.

Notice that God didn't strike the midwives down for not telling Pharaoh the truth and for making up that whole "vigorous" thing.

They could have answered, "We didn't kill those babies the way you told us to—and you know what? We're not gonna. You may be a cold-blooded baby killer, but we won't take part in it—even if you *are* Pharaoh. Sorry, God outranks you." That's what I would be tempted to say. But that "vigorous" thing seemed to work fine.

I want a family of my own. You too? Fear God. Obey Him. There's a good precedent that God will bless you as He did Shiphrah and Puah.

How will we be blessed if we fear God?

Blessed is every one who fears the LORD, who walks in His ways. When you eat the labor of your hands, you shall be happy, and it shall be well with you. Your wife shall be like a fruitful vine in the very heart of your house, your children like olive plants all around your table. Behold, thus shall the man be blessed who fears the LORD. (Psalm 128:1–4, NKJV)

I'm not one of those people who believes in changing the Bible to make it gender neutral. We should leave God's Word alone. But I don't think God is making this promise only to men. He doesn't exclude women from His blessings. Just ask Shiphrah and Puah.

If we want a spouse, and if we want children like olive plants, then we need to *fear* the Lord. Put Him first. Just as Shiphrah and Puah put God over Pharaoh, we need to put God over this area of our lives. Is finding a husband more important to you than God is?

Jesus said to seek *first* the kingdom of God, and "all these things will be given to you as well" (Matthew 6:33). That's the order.

Scripture doesn't say that God will fulfill the desires of only those who are married. Or those who fear Him *except* if you want to be married. It says, "He fulfills the desires of those who fear him; he hears their cry and saves them" (Psalm 145:19). "God sets the solitary in families; He brings out those who are bound into prosperity; but the rebellious dwell in a dry land" (68:6, NKJV). That's reason enough for me not to rebel.

And here's a reason to stop crying: "This is what the LORD says: 'Restrain your voice from weeping and your eyes from tears, for your work will be rewarded,' declares the LORD" (Jeremiah 31:16). Rewarded how? Maybe as Shiphrah and Puah were rewarded.

DESIRES OF THE HEART

I often turn to the verse that promises God withholds "no good thing...from those whose walk is blameless" (Psalm 84:11).

God is the one who said it is "not good" for man to be alone (Genesis 2:18). So I have to think that it *is* good for man to be with someone. Not just anyone, but the someone created just for him: "Then the LORD God made a woman from the rib he had taken out of the man, and he brought her to the man.... God saw all that he had made, and it was very good" (Genesis 2:22; 1:31). So if a spouse is a good thing, and He won't withhold any good thing from those whose walk is blameless, then I'm going to work to walk blamelessly. Proverbs 18:22 says, "He who finds a wife finds what is good and receives favor from the LORD." I assume that also holds true for a husband. When I pray for a spouse, I'm praying for what God says is good. That gives me confidence— because when I'm praying in God's will, there's a lot better chance my prayers will be answered.

King David praised God by saying, "You open your hand and satisfy the desires of every living thing" (Psalm 145:16). Hey, *I'm* a living thing. That means He'll satisfy *my* desire, doesn't it? And David's son Solomon said, "Two are better than one...if one falls down, his friend can help him up" (Ecclesiastes 4:9–10).

As I said, I hate waiting. So I remind God, as David did, "Remember how short my time is" (Psalm 89:47, NKJV). I would've added an exclamation mark to that! "It is time for you to act, O LORD" (119:126). I *like* that one—right along with this: "What the wicked dreads will overtake him; what the righteous desire will be granted" (Proverbs 10:24).

The truly great thing is that we can count on all these promises. Psalm 119:160 tells us clearly that all God's words are true. And God is going to make sure His Word is performed: "The LORD said to me, 'You have seen correctly, for I am watching to see that my word is fulfilled'" (Jeremiah 1:12). After all, "God is not a man, that he should lie, nor a son of man, that he should change his mind. Does he speak and then not act? Does he promise and not fulfill?" (Numbers 23:19). In case you were wondering, the answer to that is no. He does what He says He'll do. You can count on it.

"Until now you have not asked for anything in my name," Jesus says. "Ask and you will receive, and your joy will be complete" (John 16:24).

I know what you're thinking. You *have* asked, but you haven't received, so how can it be true? James 4:3 provides us with some guidance: "When you ask, you do not receive, because you ask with wrong motives, that you may spend what you get on your pleasures." But I think John 15:7 gives us the clearest picture: "If you remain in me [Jesus] and my words remain in you, ask whatever you wish, and it will be given you." Get it? As Christ describes the relationship between the vine and the branches, He gives us the best way to get answered prayers: We need to be so close to God that His words are in us—and, as a result, we ask for the right things.

But maybe you can't understand, given your circumstances, how God is going to do what He says. His Word has an answer for that too: "Trust in the LORD with all your heart and lean not on your own understanding; in all your ways acknowledge him, and he will make your paths straight" (Proverbs 3:5–6). He'll do it. His ways are higher than our ways (Isaiah 55:9), and He is not bound by circumstances.

How is He going to direct your path? What are His ways like? There's a verse I like so much that I had it saved into my cell phone. God "is able to do immeasurably more than all we ask or imagine, according to his power that is at work within us" (Ephesians 3:20). Now, I consider myself an imaginative person. I can think up a lot of things I'd like to see happen. But God blows away my small imaginings. That, incidentally, was my prayer at New Year's, when I began to write this book. I asked God to blow me away. To show me what He can do. To reveal Himself—His plan and His power—to me in a way I have never seen before. That's still my prayer.

The good news—based on this verse alone—is that He is able to deliver. In fact, "'No eye has seen, no ear has heard, no mind has conceived what God has prepared for those who love him'—but God has revealed it to us by his Spirit. The Spirit searches all things, even the deep things of God" (I Corinthians 2:9–10). I love God, and I *can't wait* to see what He has prepared for me.

God is thinking about us. When you roll over in bed tonight, ponder that. God is thinking about you right now and loving you. "How precious are your thoughts about me, O God! They are innumerable! I can't even count them; they outnumber the grains of sand! And when I wake up in the morning, you are still with me!" (Psalm 139:17–18, NLT). That's comforting, isn't it?

THE RED DRESS

Cyndy is the kind of friend I wanted to marry my brother—just so she could be my sister. Shortly after I began writing this book, she called to thank me for a book I had sent her for Christmas, *How to Pray for Lost Loved Ones* by Dutch Sheets. I liked it so much that I bought more than fifty copies and gave one to every family member and close friend I know who is saved, along with a letter welcoming them to the "Folger Prayer Force." I have declared this "the year of the Lord's salvation" and am praying for every lost family member I have. Only now I have help. And after just a few weeks, people were already reporting how God was moving in their families. So I'm recommending it to you. I know that doesn't have anything to do with my point, but I thought it was a good idea and that you might want to try it.

Cyndy and I became friends when she and her friend Julie made me their "project"—they took me shopping and gave me a whole new look. They said my clothes were too baggy, *and* I guess I had committed the cardinal fashion sin—I wore "nude" panty hose. Didn't I *know* that nude was out, that cream was in? I'm embarrassed even to be writing this. Thank goodness they got to me in time!

I was going to a Christmas dinner for my boyfriend's law firm and needed something to wear. So Cyndy and Julie took me shopping. They talked me into buying a sleeveless (not strapless) red dress—just above the knee. It was a size four. They, and the saleslady, said the six was too big. The sizes must have been off, because I only have *two* dresses in size four—and that's one of them. So I bought it and wore it to the dinner party with perhaps the most conservative guy I have ever dated.

When I say conservative, I mean *conservative*. My friend Steve and I once planned to dress like the Amish one day for this guy. I was going to be taking an apple pie from the oven as he walked in the door, and we were going to spend the entire evening saying things like, "Wouldst thou pass the salt, Brother Steve?" But my boyfriend would've *liked* it.

Strange family, though. His mother was a state legislator and one of the proabortion leaders in the Statehouse, where I lobbied for the Right to Life. No kidding. She was the one who tried to kill my bill banning partial-birth abortions.[2] Almost got away with it, too. This woman considered me her nemesis. After all, I had foiled her plans to kill our bill. Sounds kind of like a comic strip, doesn't it? Yet her son Daniel was a conservative, pro-life Christian. When Daniel said he was driving to Columbus to see me, his mother assumed he was going to one of those "terrible anti-choice" functions to hear me speak. His response was somewhat less than welcome.

"She's not speaking anywhere, Mother. I'm driving to Columbus to take her to *dinner.*"

Now, I'm not saying that I wouldn't have been welcomed into the family with open arms, but I remember exactly his mother's response: *"Tell me you're not dating Janet Folger!"*

I imagined her head spinning all the way around when she said this, but I never mentioned that to Daniel.

She eventually warmed up to me—not to my pro-life position, but she loved her son and was kind to me because of him. I have to give her credit for that.

Well, back to the red dress. I want you to know that I'm a very conservative dresser. And there was nothing wrong with this dress. As Cyndy kept saying, "It's something Nancy Reagan would wear." But Daniel didn't like it. He didn't like the fact that it was sleeveless. He thought it was too short.

Should've gone with the Amish number.

When I went with him to the ice cream social for Senator Mike DeWine (a good pro-life friend), the big event for every Republican in the state, I wore a peach dress that went almost to my ankles. Daniel thought it was "stunning." He went nuts over this dress. Couldn't say enough about it. I said, "I take it you like it better than the red one."

"Oh, yes! That thing was *way too short.*"

I just got it out of the closet, lest you think I'm exaggerating: it measures exactly an inch and a half from my knee. *An inch and a half.* We alternated words to describe a dress of that length (me—joking; Daniel—*not!*): "the best in tart wear; trollop attire; a floozy frolic..." I think we were up to the word *hussy* when we bumped into his mother—wearing a dress that had to be six or seven inches above her knees.

I complimented her on her dress and smiled as I caught Daniel's eye. Suddenly all those adjectives he had used to describe my red dress didn't seem so funny to him. I, on the other hand, found the whole thing hysterical.

WHERE'S GOD IN ALL THIS?

Cyndy called recently and asked me about God's promises. Are they really for us *now*—or do all these blessings only kick in after we die? She was serious. She is a gorgeous woman and had thought God would have given her a husband by now. For some reason, He hasn't.

I told her that I think God's promises are for *now*—except perhaps the "streets of gold." Look at Psalm 27:13 (NKJV): "I would have lost heart, unless I had believed that I would see the goodness of the LORD in the *land of the living.*" That's *now.* So what are we to do? The following verse may provide the answer: "Wait on the LORD; be of good courage, and He shall strengthen your heart; wait, I say, on the LORD!" (v. 14). The New International Version says, "I am still confident of this: I will see the goodness of the LORD in the land of the living" (v. 13). David was confident, and I believe we can be too.

Here's what Jesus said: "I tell you the truth...*no one* who has left home or brothers or sisters or mother or father or children or fields for me and the gospel *will fail to receive a hundred times as much in this present age* (homes, brothers, sisters, mothers, children and fields—and with them, persecutions) and in the age to come, eternal life" (Mark 10:29–30). Follow Jesus and you will be rewarded in this present age.

I told Cyndy that I believe I'm not married yet because God has some things for me to do while I'm single. I got a call last week from a woman who read *True to Life.* She tried an idea I wrote about—a creative way to let women considering an abortion see their babies as babies, rather than as problems. I suggested handing out sleepers—those soft, cuddly little outfits babies wear—at an abortion mill. Well, this lady called because she had just tried it, and a woman she gave one to came back out of the abortion clinic saying she'd told the "counselor" inside that she had changed her mind. She had the sleeper in her hand. Cool, huh?

I'm not sure I would have been able to do the kinds of things I've done had I been married. If something you had a part in helped to save a life, would you say waiting was worth it? I think so. But I have to admit: *Now* I'm ready to move on to the next phase—getting involved in something God can do through me *and my husband.*

Cyndy asked, "What about our friend—she's in her forties and not married, but would like to be. What about *her?*" I don't know. How's that for an answer? (You can try now for that refund on this book!) One thing I *do* know is that our friend only recently became a Christian. Imagine if she had gotten married before that. She likely would have married someone who didn't know the Lord either. Imagine getting saved *after* your marriage but having a husband who wasn't interested in God. I know people in that situation, and let me tell you, their lives are really tough. Worse than when they were waiting. Maybe that's why our friend hasn't found her husband before now.

Is there a Mr. Right? Since starting to write this, a lot of people have advised me to say there is no Mr. Right. I don't think I can, because I really don't know that I believe it. The way I see it, if God knows the number of hairs on our heads, then I'm sure He's up to speed on the rest of the details. David said that God's eyes "saw my unformed body" while it was still in the womb and that "all the days ordained for me were written" in God's book "before one of them came to be" (Psalm 139:16). If He had my days planned before He formed me in my mother's womb, I'm thinking that also includes my wedding plans. "The things you planned for us no one can recount to you; were I to speak and tell of them, they would be too many to declare" (Psalm 40:5). God has so much planned for us that we couldn't even list everything.

Why wouldn't something as important as this be on the list?

Maybe there are a couple of different people we could be happy with. But what do *I* want? I want God's best, and I'm inclined to think He has one. A man after God's own heart—that's who I want to win mine.

What we need to watch out for is mistaking Mr. Right for "Mr. Right Now." They're not necessarily the same guy. I want God's pick, not mine. He knows the future. He sees the heart. And if there's one thing I've learned, it's that I can't rely on my feelings. My picks haven't been so great. I'm going to keep my focus on Him before "Mr. Right Now" pulls me in the wrong direction!

Then Cyndy asked me about Mary and Martha. As far as we know, neither of them was married, and Jesus didn't seem to do anything about it. My answer? Well, if Jesus could raise their brother from the dead, I'm sure finding husbands for them would have been a piece of cake.

Marriage is an important thing in the Bible. Jesus went to weddings—it was at a marriage feast that He performed His first miracle. And Jesus spoke of a "bridegroom coming for His bride" as an analogy for Him coming back for His church. Marriage matters to God.

The Bible is also filled with lessons about marriage. Solomon, for example, might have been the wisest man alive, but he blew it when it came to women. Marry foreign wives and the next thing you know you're building temples to their gods. That's not so smart. The wrong woman will bring you to absolute ruin. Just ask Samson. But so will the wrong man.

And what about what Paul said about marriage? "An unmarried woman or virgin is concerned about the Lord's affairs: Her aim is to be devoted to the Lord in both body and spirit. But a married woman is concerned about the affairs of this world—how she can please her husband. I am saying this for your own good, not to restrict you, but that you may live in a right way *in undivided devotion to the Lord*" (1 Corinthians 7:34–35).

I heard a sermon from Dr. D. James Kennedy about this and felt encouraged by his take on the matter. During the time of Paul's writing, Christians were being persecuted. For those with wives and families, it was especially hard to stay strong. It's hard enough to die for your faith, but to watch your wife and children be put to death would be even harder. Yet even with those circumstances, Paul said to the unmarried and the widows, "It is good for them to stay unmarried, as I am. But if they cannot control themselves, *they should marry*, for it is better to marry than to burn with passion" (vv. 8–9). It seems to me Paul is saying that if you really want to be married, then you *should* be married. It's not only okay; it's what you should do.

FROM OBSCURITY TO ROYALTY

Esther

And what about a little orphan girl named Esther? God provided for her to be raised by her godly cousin Mordecai, who had a similar perspective that God was in control of who Esther would marry. It wasn't that she was "lucky enough" to win a beauty contest and ended up marrying the king as a result. God placed her where she was so she could go to her husband and have a hand in saving the Jews. Mordecai told Esther, "'And who knows but that you have come to royal position *for such a time as this?*'" (Esther 4:14).

Not only did God honor Esther as queen; He used her mightily for His purpose. That's what I want. Not necessarily the "queen" part—but I'm not ruling anything out.

Abigail

Then there was Abigail, whose husband, Nabal, was described in glowing terms: "He is such a worthless man that no one can speak to him" (I Samuel 25:17, NASB). Nabal had refused to help David and had even insulted him. To keep her household from destruction, Abigail went to David with food her husband wasn't inclined to share. Later, when her husband had what appears to have been a heart attack and died, David proposed to and married Abigail. So because Abigail humbled herself and did what was right, God not only got her out of a horrible marriage, but He gave her a man after His own heart.

David was a great man. A godly man. Almost *exactly* like the guy I want. Strong, courageous, sensitive, a songwriter, poet. *Loved* the whole Goliath thing. But—and maybe I'm too picky—there are a few things that would have disqualified him from my list of potentials. Multiple wives? Sorry. I'm out. I would have a problem with that whole Bathsheba thing as well. Apart from that, he'd be perfect.

Ruth

Remember Ruth? Her husband died and she remained loyal to her beloved mother-in-law, Naomi. She chose Naomi's people and Naomi's God—the God of Israel. And it was Naomi who came up with the way for Ruth to meet Boaz: "Wash and perfume yourself, and put on your best clothes. Then go down to the threshing floor...." (Ruth 3:3). Okay, the lying-down-at-the-feet-of-Boaz thing may seem a bit odd. But that was the custom. *We* get ourselves a makeover, buy a new dress, and go out to dinner. *They* got a makeover, put on a new dress, and lay down at the guy's feet. I'll stick with dinner, thanks.

But at least take note of this: Ruth didn't wait at home until Boaz showed up at her door. She followed her mother-in-law's advice to go out and meet him. God worked through her action and blessed her: "So Boaz took Ruth and she became his wife. Then he went to her, and the LORD *enabled her to conceive*, and she gave birth to a son." (Ruth 4:13).

Did you catch that? It was the *Lord* who provided Ruth with a husband and enabled her to conceive. He's involved in that kind of thing. It was God who didn't leave her a widow. And Boaz's name *was* famous. Ruth's son Obed was the father of Jesse, the father of David. That's the line from which Christ—*the King of kings*—was born.

I'm sure God was involved in all that.

Pretty in Pink

Just because you haven't found the one who's perfect for you doesn't mean you can't have fun in the meantime. I told you about the red dress; now let me tell you about my ball gown. I was asked to the Governor's Ball and had a blast—even *before* I got there. For some reason, everyone wanted to see my dress. It really was beautiful, and I felt like a princess in it. I mentioned I was going to get it fitted, and two of my friends showed up—one along with her husband and two kids.

My boyfriend was coming to see it too, and my friends and I got an idea—we went through the store and picked out the ugliest dress we could find. It was pink and green, long in the back, short in front. With ruffles all over. I couldn't stop laughing as I tried it on. Then we got the seamstress in on it. She was pinning up the bottom when my boyfriend walked in.

Of course I made it clear that I had already *purchased* the dress, and now it was being altered. There was no going back. My friends made a fuss over just how beautiful the green ruffles looked with the pink. One of them, Teresa, scurried around the store looking for accessories. I pointed out to my boyfriend that I couldn't decide whether to go with a long dress or a short one, and this way I had *both!* I looked up at his face and saw a man in shock.

The seamstress played her part well—talking about how I was a "spring" (or maybe it was a "summer") and how the pink was the perfect color with my skin tones and, of course, the green offset it nicely.

Finally I asked my date, "Well, what do you *think?*"

I remember him putting his hand on his face and saying it was "very interesting." That was when Teresa came back with the "perfect choker necklace"—even more hideous than the dress.

Even by biting my lip I couldn't suppress the laughter, and we all lost it.

The perfect guy for me won't break it off after a stunt like that! Somewhat of a tall order, I know.

We now return to a spiritual thought already in progress....

GOD'S DIRECT INVOLVEMENT...

...with Sarah

Think God isn't listening because He hasn't answered your prayers yet? Imagine how Sarah must have felt. Abraham is a hundred, Sarah is ninety, and they are childless. When he gets done laughing over God's promise that they will have a son, Abraham points out the small matter of the age issue to God. That's when God tells him, "Yes, but your wife Sarah will bear you a son, and you will call him Isaac" (Genesis 17:19).

He is God, after all. And when God says it, you can trust it. It's as simple as that. "Now the LORD was gracious to Sarah as he had said, and the LORD did for Sarah what he had promised. Sarah became pregnant and bore a son to Abraham in his old age, at the *very time God had promised him*" (21:1–2). Did you catch that last part? It wasn't that God got busy with other things and just then remembered to fulfill His promise. Isaac was born at "the very time" God had promised him.

Then they were no longer laughing *at* God's promise; they were laughing for joy at God's promise fulfilled: "Sarah said, 'God has brought me laughter, and everyone who hears about this will laugh with me'" (v. 6).

...with Rachel and Leah

God has had mercy and compassion on women throughout the Bible. When Jacob was in the nasty situation of being tricked into marrying Leah in order to marry Rachel—the woman he loved— God didn't forget either of these women. Genesis 29:31 tells of God's direct involvement in Leah's life: "When the LORD saw that Leah was not loved, he opened her womb, but Rachel was barren." And in Rachel's: "Then God remembered Rachel; he listened to her and opened her womb" (30:22).

He was directly involved.

...with Hannah

When Hannah was crying her eyes out about not having any children, her husband, Elkanah, said, "Hannah, why are you weeping? Why don't you eat? Why are you downhearted? Don't I mean more to you than ten sons?" (1 Samuel 1:8).

I know what you're thinking. *She may not have had any children, but at least she had a good husband!* I know, but read on so I can make my point. "In bitterness of soul Hannah wept much and prayed to the LORD. And she made a vow, saying, 'O LORD Almighty, if you will only look upon your servant's misery and remember me, and not forget your servant but give her a son, then I will give him to the Lord for all the days of his life" (vv. 10–11).

Maybe *you've* been crying out to the Lord lately. In misery, weeping, just like Hannah.

Watch what came next: "The Lord remembered her. So in the course of time Hannah conceived and gave birth to a son. She named him Samuel, saying, 'Because I asked the Lord for him'" (vv. 19–20).

"The Lord remembered her." He listened to her anguish and grief and *remembered* her. If He can see *her* pain and her anguish, what makes you think He can't see yours? And if He will answer her with the desire of *her* heart, what makes you think He won't give you the desire of *your* heart?

We're not asking for something that isn't in line with God's Word. He's the One who came up with the whole concept of marriage. It's His invention, His *design.* He's the One who said, "'It is not good for the man to be alone. I will make a helper suitable for him'" (Genesis 2:18).

If we pray for something that would be bad for us, I wouldn't expect God to answer in the affirmative. At least I *hope* He wouldn't. Although He *did* give Israel a king—because they wanted one—even though it wasn't for the best. I guess we need to be very careful about what—or whom—we pray for. If God has something better for us than what we're praying for, wouldn't you like Him to make a substitution? I want God to bring me the one *He* chooses, rather than the one *I* choose.

When we pray for a mate, we're just asking for what God says is good. And I know He is all-powerful. He's in control. That means He could have already brought Mr. Right to us by now. But for some reason, He has chosen not to. I believe He doesn't have us married right now because He has something for us to do first—something for Him. During this time, He is fine-tuning us—preparing us *and* the person He's chosen for us.

If you take nothing else from this book, take this: *Use* this time. Don't let Satan steal it from you. I've wasted so much time crying over guys—I'm talking *years.* What a colossal waste. So even though you can't wait for it to pass, remember that this time is precious. Do you really want to squander it by being miserable? That's not going to bring your husband any faster. In fact, I think that's going to slow down everything—or at least make it seem that way!

God has something for you to do. And He's going to give you what He has promised. How do I know? It's the theme for this book: "So do not throw away your confidence; it will be richly rewarded. You need to persevere so that when you have done the will of God, you will receive what he has promised" (Hebrews 10:35–36).

three

Dating Mr. Wrong

Is He or Isn't He?

Sometimes a definite Mr. Wrong is easy to recognize right from the start—like the guy from New Jersey I dated. Kind of ruined the whole state for me. He took me to the last of the Indiana Jones movies on opening night, and the theater was packed. As we sat waiting for the movie to begin, this really tall guy sat directly in front of me, blocking off most of the screen. I asked my date—reasonably, I thought—if he would switch seats with me since he was taller. To my astonishment, he said no. If we switched, he added, then *he* wouldn't be able to see.

Now, I was always under the impression that when a guy asks you out, he's kind of hoping you'll *like* him. Kiss goodnight and all that. Not this guy. He didn't care—as long as he had a good view of Harrison Ford.

Here's where it got fun. Because the theater was so crowded, the ushers directed everyone to move all the way over to the right of their row. Divine justice swooped down, and the really tall guy ended up—you guessed it—directly in front of my date. I was *lovin'* life! You should have heard me during the movie: "The cinematography is spectacular! The scenery...magnificent! If there is anything you'd like me to *describe* for you, just let me know." What a fun night!

Other relationships aren't so cut-and-dried. Some guys will not only willingly change seats with you, but will also get up in the middle of the movie because they see you're out of Coke. And yet they're still not the right one.

I dated a guy who was really great at making up. Just when I thought I never wanted to see him again, he'd show up at the airport with balloons and flowers and a sign that said "I'm sorry." It took my neighbor Jeff to point out that the words "I'm sorry" were on every bouquet this guy sent. And he sent them a lot. He had a bit of a temper and often said things he later regretted. That got old pretty fast. But it started off fun.

I met him at a political party and thought he was perhaps the best-looking guy I had ever seen.

He found some "official" reason to call me for lunch. Said he was so nervous that he swallowed a lemon seed that day. *Cute.* We started dating and a girl in my office discovered that if you looked out one of our office windows, you could see directly into his. She used to take "diet Coke breaks" there—to scope him out. So one day I called him from my office and complimented him on what he was wearing. Asked him if he was warm—as his jacket was hanging on his door. Then someone dropped off something on his desk—of course I had to comment. I watched him look around, wondering how I knew everything that was going on.

Later, when he was mad at me, he would close the blinds.

I did some really neat things with this guy, which always makes it hard to break up. The more memories you build, the tougher it is to break that bond, and the more willing you are to overlook the warning signs. Yeah, he's got a temper, but he's really sorry he was mean—look at how sweet he is now. Your friends may see the problems, but you don't. And when your parents bring up their concerns, you find yourself defending the guy—because they don't know him the way you do. Or maybe, just maybe, everyone else isn't blinded the way you are. The signs keep popping up, but you choose to ignore them and focus on the good things and the fun. And if he makes you laugh, he's *really* going to be hard to give up.

On one occasion, I was at the Grand Canyon with a group of friends, including my boyfriend Bob. We were at Plateau Point—halfway down the canyon on the edge of a two thousand-foot drop to the Colorado River. We met some other hikers and hit it off—found out where they were from, started taking each other's photos. I'd seen a cliff that looked as though it dropped thousands of feet to the tiny canyon floor, but actually fell only a few feet. So they took my picture there—looking as though I'd jumped off the cliff. It hung in my office for a long time with the caption: "Clinton elected; Folger jumps off cliff." *Cute, huh?*

Well, in the middle of this "cliff-hanger" escapade, with sharp drops all around us, I thought it was time to have a little fun with our new friends. I looked up at Bob and said, "Where's little Bobby?"

Of course, there was no little Bobby, but they didn't know that. They were *horrified.* Any child who was not in sight was probably on the jagged rocks below.

Bob didn't miss a beat. "I thought *you* had him."

Then we kind of shrugged our shoulders, and I said, "Well, I'm sure he's around here *somewhere.*"

Bob added nonchalantly, "Yeah, he'll turn up. What could've happened to him? You guys want more pictures?"

They couldn't answer, because their jaws were scraping the ground. I'm not sure they thought it was funny—but Bob and I laughed all the way to the bottom of the canyon.

Fun guys are really hard to break up with.

I once dated a guy for seven years (on and off—*mostly* off) because we had so much fun together. I'll never forget one fight we had—I wanted out and was brutally honest. We were going on a trip to visit friends of his. I felt that not only was the trip a mistake, but so was the whole relationship.

He could tell something was wrong and asked what I was thinking.

"I feel like we don't belong together. We don't get along. I want to break up, but now I'm locked into this trip with you, and I don't want to go."

His response? "But *other than that* everything else is okay—right?"

How can you not love a guy like that?

Another year gone.

History together is another binding influence. When you need to talk, how much easier is it to talk to someone who already knows the situation instead of starting from scratch? Your boyfriend knows all about the problems at the office, your family, your hopes, your dreams, and when you most need a hug.

I've fallen into this trap. Most of us have. It's easy. It's comfortable. And women have the uncanny ability to rationalize that, somehow, there's a chance for a future with this guy. After all, we've already invested so much time in him.

A friend of mine has been living in this trap. She's dating a guy she knows she can't marry. Why? Well, for starters, he's not a Christian. The preliminary disqualifier. The red flag of red flags. She knew it when she started dating him, but she ignored it.

For the last several years, our conversations have gone like this:

"Are you still seeing Jay?"

"No, Jan, I broke it off. I know it can't go anywhere, and I told him on Tuesday" (for the umpteenth time).

"How'd he take it?"

"Not so well. He's *such* a great guy. He's sooo sweet...."

"Yeah, yeah, I know, but he's still not a Christian, right?"

"No. But I gave him another book, and he said he would read it."

"But you broke up with him this time, right?"

"Right."

"He's at your place now, isn't he?"

"Well, yeah."

"Thought so."

Don't get caught in this trap. If the guy's not a Christian, you have no business dating him. It's like getting mixed up with a married man. I don't care *how* wonderful he is; he's off-limits.

I've been friends with Jim since sixth grade. When he got married, that changed, which was fine. But after his divorce he called me to have dinner. Turns out he experienced this phenomenon firsthand. His wife started going to lunch with a guy "friend" in her office. They spent more and more time alone together, and Jim got a bit wary of the whole matter. He told his wife that he didn't want her to see this male coworker alone. She wouldn't budge. *She* wasn't doing anything wrong, and she could have whatever friends she wanted.

We have to remember that some things inevitably happen in this situation—regardless of our intentions. The more time you spend with someone of the opposite sex, the more you share with each other, the more you're going to develop feelings for each other, even if you're *both* God-fearing Christians. That's where the whole "lead us not into temptation" thing comes into play—even though you don't feel tempted up front and it doesn't seem that there is any good reason why you shouldn't be able to spend time with someone you like and whose company you enjoy. After all, you know married guys are off-limits, and if they know it too, what's the harm?

Ask Jim.

Sure, his wife didn't keep going to lunch with this guy because she *wanted* to break up her marriage. But here's how a conversation often plays out. She talks about the problems she's having in her marriage—because there are problems in every marriage and it's just a matter of time before the subject comes up. His response to whatever she was complaining about? Well, he would *never* do that! Of course not. *Duh.* And suddenly, the grass starts looking a lot greener.

She divorced Jim and married this other guy. Now she's divorced from him. Because while maybe he would "never do that," he would do a hundred other things—many of them even worse. She got sucked into the trap and now wishes she hadn't let it destroy her family.

This happens to women every day. Remember who Satan is. That's right—he's a liar. His sole purpose is to destroy you and all the incredible things God has for you. Here's the good news: He's been using the same old tricks for thousands of years. When you know where the dangers are, it's a whole lot easier to avoid them—don't you think?

Just as you must not get sucked into falling for a married guy (don't even spend enough time with him to find out how wonderful he is), you can't let yourself fall for a guy who isn't a Christian. Some things are nonnegotiable.

I know that some women have led their boyfriends to God and then end up living happily ever after, but that's the exception. It happened to my friend Lil, who led her boyfriend to the Lord about forty years ago, and her husband has been on fire for God ever since. That's why she didn't really see a problem with fixing me up with a doctor who probably wasn't saved.

I remember our conversation at the country club—he asked me what I did for a living, and I told him how I'm involved in just about every conservative social issue from the Right to Life to Christian liberties. I could see that he was blown away by probably the most conservative person he'd ever met—not to mention the first blind date who ever walked in late, straight from work, talking on a cell phone with Day-Timer in hand. Later Lil had to remind me of that—I don't remember what was going on at the time, but I *know* it was important and couldn't wait. I was kind of upset that Lil had fixed me up with the guy—he probably wasn't even pro-life. *What was she thinking?* After listing the litany of things I've been involved with, I looked at Lil with a smile and added, for good measure, "I'm also against surrendering American sovereignty to the United Nations."

Suddenly my date remembered he had to be somewhere. Which was perfectly fine with me. It was a nice meal, and I went back for seconds.

You have absolutely no business falling in love with someone who isn't a Christian. But you can't help it, you say? I think you can find out on the first date where the guy is spiritually. If he's open to discussion on the subject, by all means discuss it. Here's a quick and easy way to tell. Ask him: "If we were in a car accident on the way home from dinner and died and Jesus asked you, 'Why should I let you into heaven?' what would you say?" After he answers, tell him what you'd say.

If he says he thinks he's a pretty good person (after all, he never killed anyone) or that he believes in God and goes to church, well, according to the Bible, that doesn't cut it. Even the devil believes in God, and he's not going to heaven. Salvation, on the other hand, looks like this:

* Recognize that you're a sinner (Romans 3:10). We can't make excuses or blame others and our circumstances for our actions (v. 23).
* Recognize that Jesus died on the cross for your sins (Romans 5:8; 6:23).
* Repent of your sins. *Repent* means to change direction (Acts 3:19). God commands us to repent and turn away from things that displease Him.
* Receive Jesus as your Savior. Don't try to clean up your life first. Come to Jesus just as you are and allow Him to change your life (John 1:12; 6:37).
* Pray: "Dear Lord Jesus, I know that I am a sinner and am in need of forgiveness. I know that You died on the cross to give me that forgiveness. I accept the ultimate gift You gave to pay the penalty for my sins. I invite You to be my Savior and the Lord of my life. I trust You and want to follow Your way all the days of my life. In Your name, amen."
* Know for sure that you have eternal life (Ephesians 2:8–9; I John 5:12–13).

If you haven't prayed like this before, now's the time. It's the most important thing you can do—and the most important thing you can do to be in God's will. If you want God's best, first you have to trust Him—completely trust Him—which means spending time in His Word, getting to know who He is and what He is like, just as you would anyone else. Talk to Him—that's all prayer is. There are no long distance charges. He will never put you on hold to take another call, put you through to voice mail, or be distracted while you're talking to Him.

Once you fully submit to God and allow Him to put you in the center of His perfect will, you're going to start seeing the plans He has for you—plans to give you "hope and a future," "plans to prosper you and not to harm you" (Jeremiah 29:11). Let God be God. We have to trust God enough to let Him do what He does best—beginning with the assurance of knowing that you have received His free gift of eternal life. That way, you can tell your date that if you were to die tonight, you know you'd go to heaven. It is solely because of Jesus taking your punishment for you that you are allowed into heaven. Jesus paid your admission price with His life.

Take your hands off the steering wheel of your life and let God start driving. I know how hard this can be, because it might not seem that God is following the plan we're just sure is best. And, well, as I told you when we first started talking in the coffee shop, I have a huge problem with His timing. I've discussed it with Him. It went something like this: "God, to *you* a thousand years may be just like a day, but *I* don't have that much time. You say You're not slow in keeping Your promises, but it sure seems that way, so can You please hurry it up?"

Besides, when we're waiting, a day *is* like a thousand years. That's why we have to quit waiting and start fulfilling the purpose God has for us.

If God's plan for me right now—before I get married—is to write this book to help single people, then that's what I want to do. If He's waiting for me to obey Him before He brings me my husband, then that's what I'm going to do. Who wants to read a book on singles by someone who's happily married? I think it must be kind of like childbirth—once you're holding that sweet little baby, you forget about the pain it took to get there. I think married people forget what singleness is like.

It's not always fun, but the game's not over. Pro football player Bob Christian spoke at an abstinence rally in Georgia where I was speaking. He told the kids about what it was like being in pro ball. It's getting up long before the sun does and running when you'd rather be sleeping. It's practicing in the heat when you'd rather be lounging by the pool. It's running the obstacle course when you have nothing left. But think about how stupid it would be to choose short-term fun over long-term joy: choosing to sit by the pool just because football practice is hard.

Bob emphasized that if he did only what he *felt* like doing, he would've missed the incredible opportunities God has given him. He would've missed out on catching the touchdown pass, winning the game, and going to the Super Bowl. He would've thrown away the chance to use his position as a platform to tell others about God and His plan and purpose for us on this earth.

Sometimes it's hard. Face it, *a lot of times* it's hard. But that doesn't mean God's not in heaven or that He's not in control. He's orchestrating everything for the long term—and that will make the short-term pain worth it. Sometimes going through tough times is just what it takes to get the job done, and God is using all that junk to build character and perseverance and patience and all that. I don't know about you, but I want the Super Bowl—even if it takes a while to get there.

Guy-Talk or God-Talk?

Here's another colossal time waster. It happens at every stage of this process of singleness. From the "Do you think he likes me?" to the "What do you think he *meant* by that?" we spend entirely too much time talking and thinking about guys. I have replayed conversations in my mind over and over, considering every inflection and nuance imaginable. And if you'll be honest, so have you.

Think about this—when was the last time you pored over *God's* words like that? I'm not talking about the Bible class you sat through. While they went over the Greek and Hebrew meanings of the words spoken by God, your mind was probably wandering...thinking about your *guy*, not your *God*.

This has arguably become the idol of today's Christian woman. Oh, we don't see it that way. All we're doing is debriefing our friends and trying to make sense of it, trying to analyze what's going on so we can make our next move. And there's a place for that—after all, that's what this book is about. But next time you're with your friends, try this: look at it from God's perspective.

Try—just try—to talk more about God's words instead of your boyfriend's. Analyze *those* for a change. When you think about it, God's words are going to tell you what to do more than meditating on how the guy at the coffee machine looked at you. Besides, if the guy who seems to be interested in you really is, chances are you're going to find out about it. If not, then he wasn't the kind of guy you want, anyway.

Then there's the "What do *you* think about him?" I've struggled with letting other people's opinions sway me. I've been talked out of dating people I wanted to date and into dating people I knew I shouldn't. Like a guy at one of my jobs. It was fairly obvious to everyone that he liked me. We were both involved in political campaigns, and he would finagle it so that he ended up working with me. He asked me out again and again, but I told him that I don't date people I work with, because if it doesn't work, well, you *still* have to work with them. When I told him that, he told me how much he *loved* his job. Said it was the best job he'd ever had. But if I wouldn't date him because I worked with him, he would quit.

Great. Now what?

I remember being lobbied by my boss and a board member. "Yeah, normally I would agree with you about not dating someone you work with, but not in this case. *This* guy's different. He's cute and fun and has a passion for the same things, and he's *crazy* about you. You'd be a fool not to give him a chance."

The other joined in. "I think he could be *the one.*"

In my gut I didn't think so, but I listened to their advice.

Big mistake. Yeah, he was crazy about me. Crazy being the operative word. Know how when a guy *really* loves you he might say something like "I would die for you"? Well, this guy said he would *kill* for me. Can I tell ya? I don't *want* anyone who would kill for me. *Psycho.*

I told him I didn't think it was working out, but he wasn't willing to accept that. He turned into a stalker. Camped outside my apartment overnight. Followed me on dates. Even got past a gated, guarded entry to follow me to the apartment of a guy I went out with—to spy on me and leave nasty notes on my car.

Then it got *worse.* He started making up stuff to spread around the office. Then he tried to get me fired. But finally the truth came out, and *he* was the one without the job.

Be careful who you listen to. And follow your instincts or pay the price.

Once I dated a guy from Colombia, South America. I walked outside one day to see him talking to my brother. He was trying to learn English, and my brother was anxious to teach him. I overheard my date asking, "What do you say to your girlfriend when you really want to be sweet?"

My helpful brother replied, "I usually say things like, 'Want to go to the movies, Scumbag?'" He sounded it out slowly—"scuuummmbaaag"—to make it easier for my Colombian friend to use it in a sentence of his own. *Nice, huh?*

Several people lobbied against a guy I was crazy about—lobbied *hard!* Normally we should at least pay attention to this. After all, maybe everybody else isn't wrong. But on more than one occasion

I've let this sway me, even though I loved the guy and didn't want to break it off. It seems stupid, I know, but it's easier than you think. All you need is a few girlfriends raising issues and suspicions, questioning his walk with God—based on their feelings or *their* interpretations of things they've heard him say—and you start wondering yourself. Maybe even though you're crazy about him, he's not who he appears to be. Maybe his feelings aren't as sincere as they seem. Maybe he's not a spiritual leader.

I remember breaking up with a guy after one of these sessions and being absolutely miserable. I was on the phone with my parents—who also didn't like him—and asked them again, "Do you really think I did the right thing?"

My mom said, "Yes!" There was no question in her mind.

But my dad said something very wise: "Janet, you can listen to all the people you want, but you're the *only* one who has to live with the decision. You need to follow your heart and do what *you* think is right."

I followed his advice and called the guy back. We got back together. And yes, he revealed to me what everyone else had seen. My mom was right. I *should* have broken up with him, but I had to do it because I knew it was right—not because others thought so.

Here's a good rule of thumb: While there is wisdom in many counselors (Proverbs 11:14; 15:22), if we're spending more time going to them about a situation than going to *God*, we're talking and listening to *them* too much.

The whole waiting-by-the-phone thing is another incredible waste of time. Remember the basic principle of this book: Quit watching the clock and get in the game. Don't put your life *on* hold until you have someone *to* hold.

If you're waiting for a call, you'd better have something else going on. And I'm not talking about flipping channels. Do something that will help you, something that will make you feel good—like cleaning your house. Somehow it's easier to clean knowing that you can drop it the minute the phone rings. And if it doesn't ring, at least you'll have a freshly cleaned house.

I'm also big on multitasking. While you clean, pray. Begin by thanking God. The writer of Psalm 119 said, "Seven times a day I praise you" (v. 164). If I want to be a woman after God's own heart, that's a good place to start. Thank Him for the house you're cleaning. Thank Him for the phone that allows people to call you—even though you hate it right now. Thank Him for your vacuum cleaner. Try cleaning your carpet without it.

Think for just one minute about how long God has been waiting for *you* to call Him—not just when you *want* something, but to talk with Him and thank Him for all He's done for you. Thank Him. Thank Him. And then thank Him some more.

Paul said, "I have learned to be content whatever the circumstances. I know what it is to be in need, and I know what it is to have plenty. I have learned the secret of being content in any and every situation, whether well fed or hungry, whether living in plenty or in want" (Philippians 4:11–12). Remember, Paul was in *prison* when he wrote those words. Remember also what he said in the next verse: "I can do *everything* through him [Jesus] who gives me strength" (v. 13).

My single friend Nancy, who has been divorced *and* widowed, has seen a lot in her life. She once told me, "I've seen it again and again throughout the years; God will not move in your life until you trust Him and have learned to be *content* where you *are.*"

If God isn't going to move me to the next phase until I'm content, then I want to hurry up and get content!

Stop worrying. Remember, God can change things in an instant! Don't keep wandering around the same mountain in the desert—thank Him for what you have, and then ask Him how you can be used by Him. Forget the phone for just a minute and look for where you can see Him moving—in your office, your neighborhood, your community. What is He doing that you could join?

For me, recently, it was a local battle for freedom. In Fort Lauderdale there was an attack on the Boy Scouts and their freedom of assembly. Turns out two words in the human rights code of the county charter were being used against all those who disagreed with the practice of homosexuality: "Sexual orientation." The charter said you couldn't discriminate based on sexual orientation. Sounds okay. No one's for discrimination. But those two words that said *not* to discriminate were being used *to* discriminate against the Scouts and all those who agreed with their hiring policies.

You see, the Boy Scouts didn't find it in the best interests of the young boys in their care to let homosexuals go on campouts with them. And the U.S. Supreme Court said they shouldn't be forced to hire people with whom they disagree.

I have to admit that I didn't really care much about this issue until I began to see the pattern. This debate wasn't about "live and let live." It wasn't about tolerance. It was about forcing people to accept, embrace, celebrate, subsidize, and teach something that God says is morally wrong. So much for not teaching values in the public school. The Bible calls homosexuality an "abomination" (Leviticus 18:22, NKJV). The behavior is evil—not the people trapped in it. When evil is taught to our children in school, forced on the taxpayer, and used to penalize groups like the Boy Scouts and the Salvation Army, it's time to stand up and do something.

I could fill a book with examples of this kind. Well, actually, I did. If you want to hear more, order a copy of *30 Seconds to Common Sense!* by clicking on my website www.F2A.org (while supplies last).

We now return to our previously scheduled boyfriend story, already in progress....

I met my last boyfriend during this Boy Scout petition drive. He came to a few of the events, and we started gathering petitions together at Wal-Mart stores, bowling alleys, and churches. I wasn't aware that such a mundane process could actually be kind of fun. With the right kind of person, I'm convinced that just about anything can be fun. Instead of lamenting about being alone, start doing something for God. Those are the kinds of people you're going to want to meet anyway.

Rather than just pray for God to make our communities better, we need to obey Him and step up to the plate. God works through people. Don't know why, but that's what He has chosen to do. As Ben Young and Samuel Adams point out in their book *The One*, rather than "let go and let God" we need to "trust God and get going!" That works with obedience; it works with relationships. You can't steer a parked car. Take a step in faith and obedience—because you'll meet people along the journey a lot more easily than you do sitting at home wishing things were different.

When you're involved in what God has for you to do, you can meet people who are also obeying Him—people involved in His work. That's the kind of man I want. I used to screen my dates in college by seeing which ones would help me post pro-life flyers around the school and work the pro-life information table. It was amazing just how *pro-life* guys could be when they wanted to go out with the president of Students for Life (a.k.a. me). Kind of like the guys who love doing laundry or yard work or anything else you happen to need when you're first going out.

Just wait a while and see how they really feel.

Toxic Waste

But of course, Satan is going to try to steal whatever joy you're experiencing. Last year I was at the Christian Booksellers Convention with my first book, *True to Life*. It was a cool thing—people calling me an "author" and stuff like that. I was talking to reporters and Christian book buyers by day—and crying by night, devastated by a long painful ordeal with toxic friends and an ex-boyfriend.

In the past, certain people had gone to great lengths to pursue my friendship. And I was beginning to see a pattern. These women would fight over who *got* to pick me up at the airport at two in the morning. That's what I'm talking about. They would bring food over and make sure they were included on every party invitation list.

Well, one of them liked the same guy I did. No big deal. That kind of thing is in God's hands, and I wasn't the least bit worried about it. At my party she followed him around all night. When he stayed to help clean up, we finally got to talk—and that's when my friend was tired. Since she was staying in the guest room, she made sure this guy and his friend had to leave so as not to keep her awake—and then she stayed up talking for another hour. After that night she started calling him and asking him to Bible studies—while at the same time disinviting me (that's right—I had previously been invited). But I've been around a long while, and this kind of stuff *never* works. It didn't matter how much my "friend" manipulated—it turned out that the guy liked *me*.

He asked me out and told me that "from the moment he first saw me," he knew that I was the one he "was going to marry." Okay, if anyone tells you this—*run*, don't walk, the other way. But I really liked him. And I'd heard of this happening with other people, so I didn't write him off immediately.

We had fun. I even grew to love his dog, a big, slobbery pit bull. I didn't like the dog at first—you hear some not-so-nice things about pit bulls—so I kept my distance. Then one day, while my boyfriend was doing something in the other room, I was on the couch half asleep, when his dog climbed up on top of me, stretched out—the length of the couch—put his head on my chest, and fell asleep. I fell in love.

When it was all said and done, I ended up missing the dog more than the guy.

Well, Mike and I were together all the time, walking the dog, making dinners, building fires—yes, even in Florida. Loving life. I started using my vacation days. But my "girlfriend" was still trying to make inroads—calling and inviting him places while he was making me dinner at his house. Mike just looked at me and said, "What should I do?" It was obvious he wanted it to stop, but neither of us wanted to hurt her feelings. She was, after all, one of my "friends."

At the same time, I was dealing with another friend who defined toxicity. She was always talking me down—I assume in an effort to make herself look better. I was trying to back away from our "friendship." She was so needy that if I told her I *absolutely* had to leave her, she would cry and go on about how she wanted to commit suicide. I spent hours telling her how bad an idea that was. I *am* pro-life, after all. It got so bad that she was pulling that little stunt at least once a week.

Are you following this? Well, even though I still liked Mike, there were things about him that I couldn't live with, so I told him that I wanted to end it. That's not what he told *everyone else*, but that doesn't matter. Even though I ended things, I was hurting. That's what happens when you care about someone.

Well, "toxic girl" apparently decided that the best way she could get back at me (for backing away from the "friendship") was to throw herself at my ex-boyfriend. Her plan was to *at least make it appear* that something was going on. Sounds too whacked-out to believe—even for me—until she later admitted it all to me. Even though nothing happened, it was her plan to make me think otherwise so it would hurt even more. A 1980s song comes to mind: *"That's* what friends are for...."

I was hurting. You know the feeling. So what did I do? I ran to the arms of my ex-fiancé. He was the only one I would rather be with than this guy. The night I called him and told him I needed to see him, I didn't know it, but he left his girlfriend sitting on his couch to come and comfort me. When he held me, all the hurt—broken relationships, broken friendships—was gone. After all, I had been loving this guy, wishing things were different, for well over a year after we broke up. He kissed me. The *chemistry* never even faded. As he pointed out, "The periodic table doesn't change." That was such a good line—it needed to be in print *somewhere.*

It helped for a short while. The operative word being *short.* It was great while we were dancing and watching the sunset in Key West together and he was telling me I was the "love of his life." *Not so great* when he was backing away to spend time with his girlfriend—who had probably been sitting on his couch all the while. So now I felt the loss of not one boyfriend, but *two.* Great plan, huh?

That's the point where I was when I called my friend Mickey from the Christian Booksellers Convention. He tried to snap me out of it. "Janet! This should be one of the happiest times of your life. You have a *book!* Do you know how many people would love to be where you are right now? And instead of being happy, you're crying in your hotel room over a relationship that isn't worth the time of day."

He was right, of course. But it doesn't feel like it when you can't get past the crippling pain to process things like facts and logic. I was able to stop crying long enough to do what I had to do there—and I had some very nice periods of distraction—but I couldn't wait to be alone again so I could cry. If I were keeping score, I would say that, by and large, Satan won that round.

But he doesn't have to. God is stronger.

Remember that.

I've wasted entirely too much time lamenting Mr. Wrong, but I know it doesn't have to be that way. I have a long way to go, but I've learned some lessons. I really want to look ahead and not behind. I'd rather be like my friend Linda—spending a short while without dates and then finding my husband—than dating all the wrong ones. I want to focus on what God has for me, rather than on what I don't have. Because it's about *Him*—though sometimes it's easy to forget that.

HAWAII: ONE FOR GOD

I once went on a business trip to Hawaii. Not bad, huh? I went to help "save marriage." If I don't get married, I'm sure doing a lot of work for *other* people. This was a few years ago, when Hawaiians were voting on whether to redefine marriage to include homosexual relationships. Now, I believe marriage should be as God designed it: the sacred union between a man and a woman. Thankfully, the voters of Hawaii agreed by about a seventy to thirty margin. But when I was there, the polls showed that it could've gone either way.

Anyway, I was asked to fly over to help. Most of the meetings weren't until the afternoon and evening. That left me with the day to play. The first day I didn't have any meetings scheduled, so I went to Waikiki Beach. Spectacular! I was *loving* life—planning campaign strategies all the while, of course.

Now you have to remember what I pointed out in the very first chapter: God has a mission for you right now that is critically important to His plan. My mission? Work to save marriage. That's what I was there to do. The scenery, the sun, and the surf were God's incredible bonus—a gift that anyone in her right mind would be thrilled about. I could have just as easily been working for marriage in Detroit, but it wasn't on the ballot there—yet. (Not that there's anything wrong with Detroit. It's a fine city with fine people. The beaches just aren't as nice.)

Satan had to come up with a way to stop me. And make no mistake, to thwart what he knows you could do for the kingdom of God, he will pull out every stop.

Step back and see how he works:

I'm walking down Waikiki Beach in awe of God's creation. The beach *and* the mountains—this place has it all. And I'm here for free, doing what I love, and Satan's plan is to try to spoil it. Which includes hitting below the belt. Though he can't read our minds, he can shoot thoughts into them. Thoughts like, *Look at all the couples. Look how happy they are! And you're here on a business trip! How* pathetic.

I don't want to give Satan all the credit here. We help him a whole lot. What kinds of things do you say to yourself? Remember, you *must* replace the lies with God's truth—something

I didn't do while at the Christian Booksellers Convention.

That's when you need to open up the Psalms and let God's truth take the place of all the lies you feel. You're not alone—even though all the physical evidence tells you so. God is the director, and even now He is working the script for your good.

So after walking Waikiki Beach all day and seeing couple after couple, hand in hand, I went back to my room alone, just as the sun was setting. I'm not sure if you know this, but it's not *just* the beach—every living person in Hawaii is on his or her honeymoon. It's true. At least, that's how it seemed.

The poisonous thoughts continued. *Yeah, I'll just go back to my room and see if I can write some commercials, or draft a few print ads for my meetings. Yippee. That'll be a blast. Or go get some dinner and eat it...alone.* I went to bed bummed out.

I woke up feeling the same way. Then I read my Bible and prayed, thanking God for all I had. I have found that the way to prevent Satan from winning is to focus on God and all the blessings He has given me. And you know what? My attitude changed. I remember saying to myself, "This is really stupid. I'm bummed out *in Hawaii?* The Christian Booksellers' Convention was one thing, but I am *not* going to let Satan steal my joy here."

I started the day by signing up for a free bus tour. And, yes, everyone else was on their honeymoon. They went around the group and everyone said who they were and how many days ago they got married...and then they got to me. I was determined to have fun in this tropical paradise, so I told them, *"He left me at the altar!"* I had the tickets for the honeymoon—so I decided to use them myself." You should have seen their faces! I enjoyed it, any-way. (Yes, I did confess that I was just kidding!)

I toured the island with a girl I'd met on the plane, sailed on a catamaran, and played in a band. I told you—I was going to have fun. I answered my cell phone with "Aloha" when friends called and never went anywhere without a flower in my hair.

Then I learned how to surf. What a blast. I surfed every day. My instructor, Indy, wondered if I wanted to have blond kids who were good swimmers. I told him that as inviting as that was, I was there to *surf*. I told the guys at my meetings, "Why would anyone want to do *anything else?*" I guess a lot of people there feel that way too. I sent an e-mail to the office reporting how tired I was at the evening meetings after surfing and shopping all day. *Something* was going to have to give—*no more evening meetings!*

They didn't think that was too funny.

Yes, Satan will try to spoil even a business trip to Hawaii—if you let him. The way to prevent it is by focusing on God. Trust Him. He had a purpose for my being there, and He was gracious enough to let me have a good time.

If you find that Satan is stealing your joy, pray for joy. As you submit to God's timing, ask Him to give you joy in the meantime—joy right *now*—when things aren't as you'd like them to be. There are a lot of good things about being single. Ask God to remind you of them—right now. Pray for fun, for laugh-ter, for balance, and most of all for joy. That's what I'm doing, and it's working.

Be Joyful

* The Lord your God will bless you in all...the work of your hands, and your joy will be complete. (Deuteronomy 16:15)

* "Do not grieve, for the joy of the Lord is your strength." (Nehemiah 8:10)

* May the nations be glad and sing for joy, for you rule the peoples justly and guide the nations of the earth. (Psalm 67:4)

* Shout for joy to the Lord, all the earth. Worship the Lord with gladness; come before him with joyful songs. (Psalm 100:1–2)

* A joyful heart is good medicine, but a broken spirit dries up the bones. (Proverbs 17:22, NASB)

* "Until now you have not asked for anything in my name. Ask and you will receive, and your joy will be complete." (John 16:24)

* "You have made known to me the paths of life; you will fill me with joy in your presence." (Acts 2:28)

* But the fruit of the Spirit is love, joy, peace, patience, kindness, goodness, faithfulness, gentleness and self-control. Against such things there is no law. (Galatians 5:22–23)

* We write this to make our joy complete. (1 John 1:4)

A Little Help from My Friends…

…Deirdre

I just finished talking to my D.C. friend Deirdre. And I'm thinking, while I've berated all of us for spending too much time talking to friends and not enough to God, it's still true that friends can really help us get through all of this. Especially when they can share keen insights with us. Here's one from Deirdre's sister: She thinks that when a guy suddenly decides he's ready to get married, he looks around to see who's standing nearby and marries her. I've actually seen it happen. Well, Deirdre likes a guy who is interested in getting married. Her plan? Fly to his city and spend some serious time loitering. *Good plan.*

I met Deirdre in a cab in San Diego in 1996. *Really!* We crashed the same party and shared a cab. She offered to pay for it, and we've been friends ever since (I don't have many friends that actually *pay* for stuff). Actually, I recognized her name as she was handing forward her credit card and asked if she knew someone named Rosemarie with the same last name. Turns out it was her mother. I had worked with Rosemarie in Ohio to draft abstinence legislation. Small world. We were both in San Diego for the Republican Convention. She had an "all access" media pass, and I had a meager "alternate" pass—but I'm the one who ended up standing just in front of the podium next to Bob Dole. That was fun. Would've been more fun if we had won.

I went to the National Cathedral the following January with several thousand other people—and ran into Deirdre again. The place was so packed that they ushered us right up front, facing everyone—just behind the altar, where the priest was giving his sermon. She couldn't believe that I, a non-Catholic, was able to get "all access" even in the National Cathedral. It was nice.

...at the Dubliner

The next day, after the pro-life march, I stopped with some friends at the Dubliner, a little Irish pub, for dinner. And I ran into her again! It seemed we were destined to be friends. We had so much fun that it became a ritual. Let me give you a glimpse. The first night, I kept running into people I knew. A girl came up to the table and said, "Janet? Janet Folger? I was just thinking about you—when I ran across a picture of us line dancing in Houston in 1992!"

It went on like that for most of the night.

The next time I was at the Dubliner, Deirdre was telling some people that every time I go there, I see someone I know. That conversation was interrupted when the server came by and told us that a gentleman at the next table said he knew me and bought my table the next round of drinks (Pepsi for all). I asked her to point him out—and it was the mayor of Columbus, Ohio, who was there as president of the National Council of Mayors meeting.

I'm telling you all of this to set the stage for the rest of the story. The next time we were at the Dubliner, Deirdre started in again with the stories. Just then, two guys walked by the table, and I was being a little silly. (Hard for you to imagine by now, I'm sure.) I looked up and said, "Excuse me, but is either one of you from

Ohio? I feel like I should know you—I'm at *the Dubliner*, after all."
As far as I knew, they were two strangers I had never seen before.

But one of them said, "I *know* you. You're Janet Folger—right?
I work for Congressman Bob Ney, and I've gone to your
Congressional Breakfast for the last two years." Deirdre thought I
was pretty cool there for a while. But she's over it now.

...at the University of Michigan Game

During that first D.C. trip when I ran into Deirdre, I met another
friend, John. We went to an anti-inaugural ball together. On the
way to the ball, we spotted a huge rocket alongside the road—left
over from the parade. Before I could say "I think we need to *own*
that," he was already making a U-turn to pick it up—I knew we
were meant to be friends. It went in the back of his truck, and he
became known around D.C. as "Rocket Man."

I visited John while speaking in Michigan in October one year.
I remember it was October because he picked me up wearing a
giant bear's head costume. I walked right up to him and said, "Hi,
John." I think he was hoping for more of a reaction.

He had a Halloween party to take me to—and three more
rented costumes from which to choose. I took the dog, and his
cousin and friend chose the frog and the chicken. He was supposed to take tickets at the University of Michigan football game
the next day, and we all went with him.

He didn't know I had experience with this. I used to work rallies when President Bush came to town—taking tickets and
anything else I felt like taking. *Really!* When you have the authority,

standing at the gate, you can get pretty much whatever you want. I told one lady, "I'm sorry, but there is no chocolate beyond this point!" People were actually handing over their candy bars! I got pizza, Pepsi, could've gotten cash if I wanted. This one guy had a really nice leather coat, and I told him, "You're going to have to leave your coat with me—you can pick it up after the rally." He started taking it off, when he saw me smiling. What a fun job!

Well, I imported all those techniques into Michigan. Sorry, Wolverines, but we also brought our costumes. Seemed like the right thing to do. These were nice costumes too—looked like the team mascot kind of thing—so we decided to be part of the half-time show. The opposing Wisconsin mascot—I think it was a gopher—was out on the field, so we thought it would be fun if we acted as though we were beating up on him. The crowd loved it! We even led them in cheers.

Then, well, there was a parade, but no animals to lead it. So we filled the void. People were lining up to get their pictures taken with us. I still remember someone saying, "Who *are* you guys? *Why* are you guys?" We were invited to the outdoor VIP cookout reception. We were hanging out of John's big old Cadillac, high-fiving the crowd. I still remember the frog head bopping to "Brown-Eyed Girl." Funniest thing you ever saw. That is, unless you saw these "animals" crowd-surfing. *That* was funnier.

We went to dinner afterward—in costume—and people came up to us all night asking for autographs. Several commented that they had seen us on the ESPN coverage of the game. This story has never gone public, but I'm hoping the statute of limitations on any laws that may have been broken has expired. Of course, I would *never* recommend doing something like that. It was irresponsible and in poor judgment. There—I hope that covers me.

As you can see, I put fun pretty high on the list when choosing my friends—and the guys I date. But the most fun guy can still be—and often has been—Mr. Wrong.

We all know what we're looking for. At the top of *my* list is the great nonnegotiable: a strong Christian leader. Remember the whole submission thing? Well, if I'm going to submit to someone, I want to make sure he's close to God and following His will. Without that, any marriage is headed down the wrong path. I want someone who prays with me in the middle of an argument. Someone who gives godly counsel—even if it goes against what I'd rather hear—without tearing me down.

PREQUALIFYING MR. RIGHT

I've had interviewers ask me if I *really* believe what the Bible says about not having sex until you're married. "Isn't that outdated and antiquated?" "Everyone is having sex." "Why would anyone in their right mind abstain?"

Want to know why? Because we serve a God who is *for* us. He came up with the whole sex idea—and He's free to set the boundaries. Because we serve such a loving God, we can trust that His rules are for our good.

I could tell you about all the sexually transmitted diseases. I could talk about the more than 40 million dead children—

aborted babies—that lie in the wake of us breaking God's commandments in the area of sexual purity. But there's another consequence you may not have thought about. What we did in the past may hurt the person we marry.

Like it or not, we carry every relationship with us into the future. And if you had sex with your last boyfriend, you have engaged in a spiritual act of unity. That's why it hurts so severely when the relationship ends. God says that two "become one flesh" (Genesis 2:24). It's like you're the *same* person. The bond is great—no matter what you tell yourself. Especially for women. That's why God says it's reserved for the one you marry.

When you don't do things God's way, there is going to be pain. I was engaged to a guy I thought was the love of my life. He was fun and thoughtful and, well, wonderful. But he was also divorced. Please don't take this as anything against divorced people—his wife cheated on him and he had biblical grounds for the divorce. He did nothing wrong. But you know what? God hates divorce for a reason: It hurts people. It hurt my boyfriend, the one who was betrayed. It hurt his little boy, perhaps most of all. And eventually it hurt me. Because besides the usual hurdles that come with any relationship, when a divorce is involved, additional hurdles are built in. Not that they can't be overcome, and not that God can't work good from them, but there they are.

Those built-in hurdles created real problems for me. Even though I loved the guy and his son, I had trouble dealing with the divorce issue. It was difficult to plan our honeymoon knowing he'd already had one.

One day, when we were talking about who we would choose for our wedding party, the painful thoughts crept back in. I asked him who his best man was going to be, wondering if it would be his brother—like the *last time*. That's when he told me he was going to choose my dad. *Brilliant move.* Now you can see why I was so in love with him.

Then there was his little boy—smart, thoughtful, and very funny. He looked like me, and wherever we went, people thought he was my son. I remember the first time I met him. I was all freaked out at the idea of becoming an instant mother, and I told my boyfriend that I didn't know if I could handle it. I felt like I had to get out. That was when this little boy came into the room and said, "I love you, Janet." My heart melted, and I fell in love with him at that moment. I wanted to be his mother. It was the whole *stepmother* thing I wasn't particularly fond of.

I didn't really care to hear about encounters with the ex-wife, which I realized were going to be a part of my life—for the *rest* of my life. I *really* struggled with it. I pictured him seeing me in my wedding dress for the first time—something you wait your whole life for—wondering if he'd be thinking about the last time he did that. *Yuck!*

Then there's the guy I just broke up with. Before he became a Christian, he slept with more people than he seemingly can count. God has forgiven him, of course. But when you don't do things God's way, somebody is going to be hurt. Then he was married, with a similar divorce situation—his wife cheated on him. Just before we broke up, he asked me to help him with his résumé. I gladly agreed. I started scrolling through the e-mail of his résumé as we talked on the phone. There was the spa he'd started with his ex-wife. Just *another* unpleasant reminder of all that I didn't want to face.

I grew quiet, and I knew he could tell what I was thinking. I said, "Maybe someone else should help you with this."

I think that's when he decided that maybe I should *see* someone else. And maybe he was right. I wasn't through trying to make it work in his case because I had already fallen for him. And while part of me was still rooting for him, I have to submit what I want to God's will. If God's best was this guy, he would have to be willing to help me through the rough times—to "love me *through it,*" as he once said. "For this is the will of God, your sanctification; that is, that you abstain from sexual immorality" (I Thessalonians 4:3, NASB).

Maybe you've never thought about this: Until the person you're dating becomes your spouse, he is likely to date and marry someone else. Chances are, you're dating someone else's future spouse. And somewhere, another woman is with your Mr. Right. What would you want him doing on his date? That's right—handshake at the door. *If that.*

Think about it. And don't defraud someone else of their spouse's purity—just as you wouldn't want anyone else to defraud your husband before you've even met him.

I was encouraged recently when talking to an ex in Phoenix. He said the same things I've felt for years and then read me the lyrics of a song he wrote for his wife-to-be—about how he has waited for her even though he's never met her. I thought I was going to cry. Good thing he didn't *sing* it to me, or I might have fallen for him all over again.

You see, I've been trying to make it work with guys who didn't do it God's way—all the time wondering if something was wrong with *me* because it hurt so much. Truth is, it's *going* to hurt. You just have to know if that's something you can handle. For me, it's been the deal breaker a number of times, particularly in the past four years. So much so that I have to consider making it a prequalifier.

Perhaps you struggle with something else. No one's perfect, and only you know what you're able to handle. A girl I worked with wouldn't date short guys. I've turned guys down because they were too tall. Nothing wrong with any of them. But I'm coming to the realization that if previous sexual experience is a recurring problem for *me*, perhaps I need to do a bit more prequalifying.

Granted, asking a guy if he's had sex might not be a first date kind of question. But if you wait, sometimes you're already in love with him by the time you find out. I need to guard my heart more until I know this is a person I could spend the rest of my life with—without having to deal with the built-in hurdles.

God forgives sin as far as the east is from the west (Psalm 103:12) and no one who has repented and trusted in Jesus is any different in God's eyes—no matter what his or her background. And there are thousands of people—arguably a majority—for whom this issue doesn't seem to matter all that much. All I'm saying is it might be time for *me* to try something else. I'm going to look for someone who loves God and has lived for Him in this area.

While we're on the subject, I've noticed some things that aren't being taught very well—like the whole concept of purity. I used to think I was doing well by not having sex. But you know what? God expects *more*. I know what you're thinking: *You've got to be kidding!* But it's true. He is holy and wants us to be holy. We are to be pure in thought and action. I haven't done nearly as well here. When you quit looking at Hollywood and the world's standards and look at God's, you can see just how much we fall short.

When we do things God's way, He will bless us. If you've found that God isn't blessing your relationships, ask yourself, "Am I doing it God's way?"

Set up some safeguards so you don't always find yourselves alone together. Trust me. I know what it's like. You want to spend every waking minute with this guy, and nothing else—or no one else—seems to matter. I've let men take the place of all of my other friends. At the time, it doesn't seem to matter much because I'm having a blast and loving life with my new best friend. He's the one I call the moment something incredible happens, the one I *have* to call when something goes terribly wrong.

But you know what happens if the relationship doesn't work out? Not only do you lose your boyfriend—not only do you lose your *best* friend—you lose the one who has become your *only friend.*

Ouch.

Set up boundaries so that you're with groups, with other couples, and yes, with single friends. Get out of your house or apartment (or his car) and make sure you have activities planned. When you have fun just going grocery shopping with the guy, it seems like a waste to pay to go to a play or ice skating, but you're better off if you do. It's good to have colorful life memories—rather than one big blur of always "hanging out." See places and do things the way you did when you were first dating. Only this time, try to include others.

When we submit to God and get in the center of His will, He can not only engage us in our mission for Him, but I believe He can also line things up for the person He wants us to be with. He may need to work on us as well as that guy He has in His perfect plan for us.

When you really think about it, isn't it much better to wait for the right guy than invest more of yourself in the wrong one? Remember, the only thing worse than waiting on God is wishing you *had* waited on Him.

My friend Andy goes nuts over every girl he dates. Dozens of roses, cards, packages. He fixes everything that's broken, makes dinner, and plans romantic outings. If he weren't so young, *I'd* marry him. But he has recently come to the realization that he's been investing in someone else's stock. It's not good to go completely overboard on someone who isn't "the" one.

I also have a tendency to do that. Once a friend and I kidnapped my boyfriend and took him to the Bahamas. He even made it through airport security blindfolded. People were taking videos of us, referring to him as "Sensory Deprivation Boy." I had the whole plane in on it—everyone yelled "Surprise!" as the blindfold came off. The flight attendant pretended we were going to Baltimore, but then announced that we had a "destination change" to the Bahamas while everyone clapped! It was just like a movie.

The problem? I broke up with him on that trip.

Oh yeah, it was worth it.

Once I talked to a boyfriend on the airplane phone. Big deal? I talked from Fort Lauderdale to Cincinnati. In case you're wondering, it cost about six hundred dollars. I think that's why Larry Burkett never had me on his show about how to manage your money.

Wrong guy. Wrong investment.

Rather than investing in someone else's stock, make your greatest investment in spending time with God. It's not always easy, but the returns will be far, far greater.

By the way, let me give you a handy little tip I've shared with a number of young women. Don't want to kiss him? Avoid that awkward time at the door by initiating a hug. *Anyone* can hug—without it meaning anything—so it's "safe." That way you don't have to kiss him, and he doesn't have to feel stupid or rejected.

Choose God's long-term plan for your life over whatever carrot Satan may dangle in front of you for the short term. The wrong guy, even if he provides short-term fun, is still the wrong guy. No matter how much time you have invested, if he's Mr. Wrong, walk away so God can give you Mr. Right. Don't misunderstand—it'll be hard. Put your focus back on God so Satan doesn't steal the joy of the blessings He's given you—like being in Hawaii—just because you're not there on your honeymoon.

Put down the Kleenex and pick up your Bible. *Do something* with the time God has given you! The sooner you do, the sooner

God can give you what He has for you around the corner. Remember, to love God is to obey Him. You love God when you actually *do* what He says. *That's* when the blessings start to flow, and Mr. Right shows up.

The Breakup

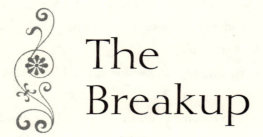

You know what it's like to hear from your married friends, whose lives seem to be all sunshine and roses, that things will soon change for you. Yeah, yeah.

Let me tell you where *I* am. New Year's Eve is just a few days away, and I may have mentioned that my boyfriend just broke up with me. So my options are Dick Clark's New Year's Rockin' Eve, four parties I have no real interest in attending, or what I wish I had done last year: eat cookie dough and take NyQuil to sleep through it all. No, I've never misused a drug like NyQuil, nor would I, but it seems like the best option right now. My friend Abby came up with the NyQuil suggestion. The cookie dough was my idea. I'm sure there are more options, but I can't think of any at the moment. Can you relate?

Just a small aside for further insight: One day at the office, a group discussing meals turned to me. "And what did *you* have for dinner last night, Janet?"

I had to be honest even though it wasn't pretty. "Cookie dough." That's what I had. That's *all* I had. And it was good.

My writer friend Bob's response was rather harsh. "That's lonely, pathetic, and slothful."

Ouch. Apparently one adjective wouldn't do. That's what happens when you work with writers.

When Bob left to become a full-time pastor, I presented him the delicacy as a going away gift. With every eye on him as he took his first spoonful, I asked, "What do you think of cookie dough now?"

"It's *economic, resourceful,* and *delicious.*"

That's what I thought.

GETTING THROUGH

There are a few ways to handle breakups. Let me tell you about one of my favorites. I broke up with a guy I had been seeing for three and a half years. Make that *he* broke up with me. I was planning to drive three hours to take him out for his birthday. I was going to do it up right and spend quite a bit of money, but he broke up with me.

So I went shopping instead. But the malls were closing. They were pulling down those metal gates. But I *needed* to shop.

I asked the girl if I could come in for just a minute to buy one thing.

"Sorry, we're closed."

You know the drill. So I complimented her on her shirt and asked if she got it there. She said yes and pointed to the display.

"Could I just buy one of those shirts? I really like it."

"No, that wouldn't be possible." After all, they were closing out the registers. Then I told her that my boyfriend had just broken up with me and I was anxious to spend some of his birthday money. When she heard that, the gate flew up and I was in.

I wasn't just in the store—I was *in!* When the girls inside heard what had happened, everything changed. Suddenly they didn't care so much about getting off work. I was paying for my shirt when I noticed other items I thought I should buy. The next thing I knew, I was trying things on. Then a few of the salesgirls were bringing me more of "this would be perfect on you." I had six girls waiting on me. I got not only what became my favorite shirt, but tons of clothes and accessories that made me feel a whole lot better.

Yeah, I know those other books won't recommend buying stuff to feel better after breaking up. But since you're my friend in the coffee shop, I'm going to tell you what's worked for me.

But wait! There's more.

One of the best things I've found for breakup recovery is a makeover. But remember, you're especially vulnerable at this time and will be easy prey for a commission-seeking makeup clerk. I once let this woman talk me into buying a bright pink lipstick. I'm talking shocking, glow-in-the-dark pink. The lady told me that it brought out the blue in my eyes. She said it was a whole new me. Well, it was. I should have checked out *her* makeup before taking her advice. Anyway, get yourself a new lipstick and maybe a new shade of blush. I'm telling you, you'll feel better.

Now get your hair done. Get it cut; get it highlighted. Doesn't matter—just make sure you leave the salon feeling pretty. And don't get the *same* thing as always. In fact, find a friend whose hair looks great and ask her where she goes. Go there and get the same hairdresser. Ask what she recommends for you, and don't be afraid. Just do it. It'll grow back.

Now you need to make some additional changes. You know how you've put God on the shelf to make time for this guy? First, confess it as sin. You've broken the first commandment—you know, the one about not having other gods before Him? Come on. You know you have. We all have. Now humble yourself and admit it.

You can never be happy putting a guy in the place of God—because he's human and will always let you down. God has to be the one you run to—because He's ultimately the only one who can satisfy your needs, rescue you from trouble, give you a true sense of self-worth, and enable you to live out all the things He has planned for you. No matter how good a guy may be, he cannot provide what God can. When you've let your boyfriend take the place of God, you've not only cheated the God who made you; you've cheated yourself as well.

But take heart. It's a recurring theme in the Bible—humble yourself and God will lift you up. "The LORD lifts up those who are bowed down" (Psalm 146:8). You've fallen (in love...and away from God?), but God will uphold you. Bow down to Him, and He will raise you up. He *really* will. It's as sure as the sunrise.

You know how you haven't gotten up early to read what God has to say to you because you kept staying out late with this guy? It's time to get back to basics—back into God's Word. Start by reading through the Psalms with a pen in hand. I practically memorized them after one breakup. They are a healing balm. All those promises are going to give you incredible hope.

Now start working out. Start getting up at five and walking before you go to work. I'm not kidding. But don't get overwhelmed. If all you do the first day is put on your shoes and walk to the end of your driveway, that's a great start. On the next day, go a few houses down. Then to the end of your block. The most important thing is that you get started.

Anything you do is a start. Even if you just put on your sweats and tennis shoes and go back to bed, which, yes, I have done. Look at it this way: Tomorrow you can actually go outside. Or get on the treadmill. Or do five minutes of your workout video. You just need to get started.

When you're out of the habit, getting out of bed early is almost impossible. I said five in the morning because that way you might make it out of bed by six. Keep trying because it will change your life.

I made a tape of upbeat songs, which helps me keep up the pace. Christian music. You're going to need that to keep your focus on God—on the fact that He's good, faithful, and powerful enough to deliver you out of your circumstances.

If you have a girlfriend in the same situation, plan to work out with her. Maybe after work or on weekends so you can hold each other accountable—until one of you meets someone new, anyway. My friends Christine and Beau used to bring exercise videos over. We made popcorn and sat in front of the fireplace and watched the videos—until the brownies were done. Then we put on a movie. Not much of a workout, not real "accountable"—but we had fun.

Try exercising in ways that aren't so tedious. Try Rollerblading, racquetball, or biking. When I moved into my first house in Columbus, Ohio, all the neighborhood kids were playing Rollerblade hockey in the street. I put on my blades and asked if I could play. At one point, a mom of one of the kids was standing outside so I asked the kids if we should invite her to play.

"No way! She'd never want to play hockey with us." "Yeah, she's old! She's like, thirty-three!" I was "like" thirty-three. But I was *cool*.

A few days later, Charlie from next door knocked on my door and asked me if I was "allowed to come out and play." I just looked at him. "I mean, uh, *can* you come out and play?"

Break out of your patterns. Do something new.

Here's another one: Use this time to make some resolutions. After you've eaten all the necessary postbreakup chocolate, change your eating habits. Get with someone who is eating right and ask for advice and accountability. I have a person like this in my life named Sharon. She's a health food nut. Vegetarian. Drinks wheat grass and this sludge called "Superfood," which I couldn't choke down. I've asked Sharon for help, but mostly for accountability. She's the one I turned to when I wanted to lose weight for my high school reunion. Whenever I was about to eat a candy bar or order something fattening, she would remind me about the reunion.

By the way, it was worth it. You know the snotty girls in junior high? One of them said to me, "You look great; you must be *loving* this." Guys who wouldn't have thought of asking me out were calling me a "hottie." Yeah, it was worth it.

You need a goal like a reunion—or an occasion when you're going to run into your ex. Eat only "live" foods (fruits and vegetables) for a week. "Life begets life," as Sharon always says. You need to feed your cells. Try to go a month. You're still gonna want something cooked—like a baked potato at dinner—but this isn't a book about nutrition, because I know even less about that than I do about relationships. Just find yourself a Sharon and change your eating habits.

When my buddy Andy came by to pick me up for the airport, he looked through my refrigerator and found nothing inviting. "Where are the cookies?" he asked.

I guess I make them a lot.

I yelled from my room, where I was still packing, "That was the old Janet." I poked out my head, held up the apple I was eating, and said, *"This* is the new Janet." He told me he liked the old Janet better. Then he rummaged through my freezer until he found some cookie dough and made himself a panful. If I'd known it was in there, I already would have eaten it—new Janet or not.

HALT

This is not the time to make rash life decisions. Remember the HALT principle: Don't make important decisions when you're Hungry, Angry, Lonely, or Tired. You're asking for trouble, especially if you fall into more than one category.

Let me address the last one first. *Tired?* Take a nap. Can't sleep? I think it's really nice that crying makes us tired. Cry yourself to sleep if you have to, but *sleep*. Too often we run ourselves ragged and wonder why everything is falling apart. Satan loves a tired target—don't give him free rein.

Hungry? Eat. Aren't you glad you paid good money for this book? Eat what's good for you, but if you mess up, don't get angry—that's the next problematic letter!

Angry? Let go. Harboring resentment only hurts you. Vengeance belongs to God, not us (Deuteronomy 32:35). Forgive the person (and yourself too) and let God handle it for you.

Lonely? That's the one that hurts the most right now. Run to God first and then get support from friends. Let them be there for you.

If you find yourself in any of these categories, HALT. Stop in your tracks, drop to your knees, and pray (not to be confused with "Stop, Drop, and Roll," which is good to remember if you're ever on fire). An emotional "fire" is not much different—wait until you have eaten, forgiven, run to God, and rested before doing or saying anything. You'll be glad you did.

My friend Mary was engaged to Fred, the love of her life. She showed everyone her engagement ring, and they set the date. They registered, decided on the guest list, and purchased what would become their marriage bed. That's when Fred told Mary he couldn't go through with it. Said he'd never loved her. That he was only marrying her because he felt sorry for her. Mary asked why in the world he'd *said* he loved her and why he went this far. His answer? He wanted to give her "temporary happiness."

That has to be a new low. Which is what I told Mary when *we* were in the coffee shop. Probably not what those other books would say, but this is my book. And, good or bad, that's what I said. I suggested that we have someone go to his house with a big check and tell him he won the Publishers Clearing House Sweepstakes. After all, that would give him "temporary happiness" until he found out the truth—not too spiritual, but it sounded right at the time.

If anyone had a right to feel depressed, Mary did. I invited her to do Beth Moore's *Breaking Free* Bible study with me. It focuses on Isaiah and how God can make beauty from ashes. Mary had ashes, and if God could make beauty from them, she was willing to try. In a restaurant one night, Mary told me she was going to take her hands off the wheel—spiritually speaking—and let God show her what He was going to do. I liked that so much, I wrote it on my napkin and decided that I wanted God to do that for me too. If Mary, who had just been through enormous rejection and humiliation, could trust God, then so could I. I decided right then that I want Him to show me what He can do.

Here's the deal: Either what God says is true, or it isn't. I happen to believe it is. That means *all* His promises are true. Every last one. Including that bit about working even the ashes of our destruction into beauty—into good.

Want to know what happened with Mary? Well, it turns out Fred was miserable without her. *Poor guy*. She told him about what she had learned in the Bible study and how she was trusting God to work everything for her good. She had always wanted to live in Nashville, but Fred wasn't willing to move. He wouldn't have thought of changing his location for her dream. So she lined up a job and moved there herself. She trusted God and took her eyes off Fred. Then Fred followed. He told her he was going to win her back and make everything up to her.

Mary, of course, asked how she could possibly trust him. He said he understood, but was determined to convince her that his love for her was real, and he wanted to marry her more than anything else in the world.

I was at their wedding. Mary looked happier than I had ever seen her. Fred understood why people were a little suspicious of him, and he promised to convince them. And he's doing it.

That's what God can do. Work all things for our good. Even when it seemed there was *no hope* of reconciliation, Mary told me that what she learned during that time was worth all the heartache. She grew closer than ever to God. She trusted Him as never before, and He proved Himself to be trustworthy. Even if Fred's heart hadn't been changed, Mary had grown to rely on God for everything. She took her hands off the wheel and told God to "show her" what He could do with the mess. Beauty from ashes— that's God's specialty. Even when the house is burned to the ground and beyond repair, God can work it for our good and rebuild the house into something even more beautiful.

Remember that He is God. That means He can do anything. Let Him show you what He is capable of.

God Is God

* The LORD answered Moses, "Is the LORD's arm too short? You will now see whether or not what I say will come true for you." (Numbers 11:23)

* I cry out to God Most High, to God, who fulfills his purpose for me. (Psalm 57:2)

* In his heart a man plans his course, but the LORD determines his steps. (Proverbs 16:9)

* Many are the plans in a man's heart, but it is the LORD's purpose that prevails. (Proverbs 19:21)

* The LORD is the everlasting God, the Creator of the ends of the earth. He will not grow tired or weary, and his understanding no one can fathom. He gives strength to the weary and increases the power of the weak.... Those who hope in the LORD will renew their strength. (Isaiah 40:28–29, 31)

* "I am the LORD, the God of all mankind. Is anything too hard for me?" (Jeremiah 32:27)

God in the Desert

Make sure you use this time in the desert to draw near to God. One of my friends told me that after her divorce she got to know God like never before. She couldn't wait to get into His Word and see His messages for her. A horribly hard year, but one in which she also grew to rely on God.

She is one of the godliest people I know. Unfortunately, many times it takes a lot of pain to get us to that point. In my friend's case, her husband had cheated on her. She took him back—and he cheated again.

As she began to suspect him, God started giving her specific verses —words of reassurance that He was there for her, that *He* would be her husband. Then, while staying at a hotel, she felt prompted to check the phone bill for any long distance charges. She called the number on her bill and got the "other" woman, but the woman wouldn't reveal anything.

This is where the story becomes like a movie or soap opera. My friend's mother called the woman, pretending to sell cosmetics. She befriended her over the phone and made arrangements to give her a free makeover. (I'm not condoning what took place; I'm just reporting it.) After the makeup session, she grabbed the woman's hand and said, "I read palms too." She studied the woman's palm. "There's a man in your life, a tall blond man (my friend's husband). And there are *four* children (my friend's kids)—am I right?"

The woman couldn't believe it. "Yes! I'm having an affair with a married man! There *are* four children! This is amazing!"

Yeah, it was *amazing* all right.

My friend's mother got the woman to tell her where her parents lived. She called them and told them what their daughter was doing. And in no time at all, she was gone.

Then her mom turned to her son-in-law. She started with his parents. Hey, it had already worked *once*. They all had a meeting about coming clean, and he finally did.

I'm guessing she got a really nice Mother's Day card that year.

My friend is now remarried to a wonderful guy. And her ex? He's repeating that destructive behavior with his new wife, and if he continues, he'll see his new family destroyed just the same.

God's rules are for our good. He will see us through the dark times and bring us to the light. That's what He does. We just need to hang on and trust Him. Draw near to God during this post-breakup time, and not only will He draw near to you; He'll also take care of you.

Now comes the nitty-gritty: You've had a makeover, bought a new outfit, changed your eating habits, and started working out. You've disarmed Satan's artillery by replacing his lies with God's truth, which you're going to have to keep doing. Keep those Bible verses close by. Better yet, get a journal and start writing down the ones that are most meaningful to you. Keep going back until you know them by heart.

Now you need to go before God. Get on your knees and ask Him what He would have you do. You now have some time on your hands you didn't have before. It's time you asked God what His mission is for you. Look at this as a divine opportunity to be in God's will, and start putting Him first in your life again.

Probably the most productive times in my life have been directly following a breakup. You have to take all that energy, all those emotions, and use them for good. The first time I read my Bible all the way through was when I broke up with Matt. After Walter, I memorized portions of Psalms just by reading them so much. When I broke up with Daniel, I did a life-changing Bible study, *Experiencing God*, by Henry Blackaby and Claude V. King. (If you haven't done that yet, go buy it and do it.)

And now, after John and Len, I'm finally writing this book. *Hooray*. I'm right with you, sister. This is *just* what I wanted to be doing on New Year's Eve. But maybe, just maybe, something I do with this time in the desert can be used to encourage someone else. Reading the first four pages (that's all I had for a few months) has encouraged me already. After all, we *all* need to be reminded that God is *for* us, working *even this* for our good, and that He has some important things for us to learn and do.

ANOTHER PIECE OF CHOCOLATE CAKE?

We're at the coffee shop—remember? And I know exactly what you're going through. Yeah, I'm trying to use this time productively. Yeah, I want to be in the center of God's will. I don't want to waste time that I could be using for God, but I have to admit that since I started writing this book I've already called three ex-boyfriends, and I'm going to dinner with one of them tonight. I know there's no future with them, and this guy tonight is just a friend, but it's not easy being alone. It's lousy.

If you do go out during this time, remember to guard your heart. We all know that guys have a way of roping us in, talking over the memories and the fun and how much they miss us. It's easy to get swept away and fall back into a dead-end relationship that doesn't get you any closer to the one God has for you. So be careful.

I know we need to have female friends, but I haven't done so well with them in the past. For example, I find that ultimate female event—the shower—to be one of the worst things to attend. What joy for a single woman—sitting for hours watching *someone else* open gifts and making small talk around recipes, cleaning products, little Johnnie's cold. *Oh boy.*

Admittedly, I haven't spent a lot of time or effort fostering female relationships. I just find guys much more fun. But here's the problem: Once they get married, their wives most often see to it that I'm stricken from their list of friends. I've lost three of my best friends that way—guys who married women they met through me!

Brian—Bri—was one of those friends. He and I used to go to Pizzeria Uno in Columbus. We had a favorite waiter there named Jim, a stocky guy who was disappointed if we didn't ask for him. So we always asked for him. As soon as we walked in, he'd put our pizzas in the oven and bring us our raspberry iced teas.

We began filling out the comment cards on the table. We would take some with us when we traveled and mail them from out of state to show how "Jim the Waiter" was touching lives around the nation—how people everywhere aspired to be like him, how he made our lives better and more worthwhile. I passed the comment cards out to my friends at a party and they wrote about how Jim had "talked them down from the ledge," "got them off alcohol and drugs," and "taught them to read between appetizers and dessert." One guy wrote that he was leaving his successful job as a stockbroker so he could follow in Jim's footsteps as a server.

We invited Jim to that party, but he had to work. That's when we called his boss and said we couldn't possibly have a party without Jim—he meant so much to each of us. Jim came. Everyone was chanting his name when he walked in. He already thought Bri and I were crazy, but he couldn't believe that we had a whole houseful of people in on the gag. People were lining up for photo ops with Jim in front of the American flag. Jim gave an impromptu speech and said he'd thought maybe he should be doing more with his life besides waiting tables, but that now, *today*, he was proud of what he did. He only wished his mother could see him. We even made a video of it all.

Of course I knew that my relationship with Bri had to change when he got married—that his wife needed to become his best friend. But to be cut out entirely seemed patently unfair. Bri's mother called me crying to tell me that I had been uninvited to his wedding. All my friends would be there—people Bri met through me—but I wasn't allowed to attend.

Kirk was another friend who would think nothing of taking a road trip to my speaking engagement in West Virginia or hanging Christmas lights with me at midnight on the tree in my front yard. When I started a band, Kirk was in it. (We only performed once at a coffee shop, but that's all we wanted to do. Kirk called us "Folger and the Crystals.") But just a few months ago, Kirk called me crying and apologizing for doing the same thing Bri had done, even though he'd *promised* he never would. I knew I couldn't pal around with him the way we did in the old days, but I always thought we could at least double-date.

UNREAL FRIENDS

Another problem has been that several of my female "friends" have turned out not to be. You know what I'm talking about. They've hit on my boyfriends—even calling them when I was around. *Nice.* "Best friends" have used me for my connections. Laurie got her husband a job through the guy I was dating, and when he and I broke up, she fixed *him* up with one of her girl-friends. The next thing you know, she used my ex and that new girlfriend to finagle an invitation to a private reception with the president (yes, of the United States). Gotta give her credit. She was *good*.

Those are people you can do without.

You know how men can sometimes be jerks? Well I'm convinced that women can be worse. If you need more proof, read on.

I had a "friend" who really sought out my friendship—and made great efforts to get into my inner circle. I'll call her Bertha (why not?). She couldn't spend enough time with me. But once she got my best friend to take her to the ball, I wasn't needed anymore, and I wasn't on the invite list. I was actually *disinvited* from a camping trip (they liked the "mix of people" they already *had* coming).

Well, as clear as Bertha made it that she was just using me, her roommate Diane made it even clearer. She was only interested in me for my male friends. She told me so up front. I thought that was nice of her.

One night Diane called from a club and asked about my guy friends. Seems they were out dancing and needed some partners. My guys, she said, were cute and fun—especially Jeff, my neighbor, and my buddy Steve.

Sure, I told her, I'd be happy to bring them along. Where did she want to meet?

Apparently I hadn't understood what she was asking. "No, Janet, I'm not talking about *you* coming. Just *them.*"

"That's pretty funny. You want me to call up all my friends to spend the evening with you guys, but I'm not invited? You're hysterical. What time should we meet you?"

"I'm *serious.*"

"You want my friends—but *I'm* not allowed to join you?"

"Right. I hope you understand. We already have enough females—we just need more males." And apparently I was the one who could provide them. Neat, huh?

I gave her Jeff's and Steve's numbers. I didn't think I should have to call them. But for some reason they both chose to come over to my place to hang out instead. The two of them launched into their routine as soon as they got in the door:

"Steve and I were talking, Jan, and we think it's a beautiful night for a drive. Can you go put some gas in your car?" At that time I had a red Alfa Romeo convertible—really fun to drive—so Jeff's comment didn't surprise me.

"Great idea," I agreed. "Let's go."

"Jan?"

"Yeah?"

"Uh, we just want you to go get the gas. Steve and I want to use the car to pick up chicks. So if you could go fill it up, that would be great."

I *loved* these guys. Two of the people in my life who could cheer me up no matter how bad things looked. I don't think there was ever a time when they couldn't make me laugh.

"Sure. I'll do that for you."

"And Jan," Steve said, "if we meet anyone, we'll need a place to bring them, so if you could be out of here before we get back, we'd really appreciate it."

Jeff added, "And can you clean up the place? We don't want these girls to think we're slobs."

"And stock the refrigerator? If we're going to be entertaining, we're going to need something to feed them."

"Just make sure you're gone."

Just like talking with Diane—only *they* were kidding!

Then there are those toxic female "friends"—the ones everyone else but you can see through. The ones who, while flattering you to your face, are talking you down behind your back. I had one of those toxic friends for a couple years. Once it was made abundantly clear to me that this was the case, an albatross was lifted from me when I removed her from my inner circle. I just wish I had listened to others and done it sooner.

To remove toxic people from our inner circle doesn't mean we're being unkind, or that we don't wish them well, or that we can't pray for them. All it means is that the inner circle is reserved for true, loyal friends who sincerely want what's best for you and will work to encourage you rather than tear you down. There's enough of that on the outside without inviting it in. It's wise to be careful: "A righteous man is cautious in friendship, but the way of the wicked leads them astray" (Proverbs 12:26).

THE REAL THING

If you've been where I have, maybe it's time you take your friend-ships to God. I did. I prayed (as has my mother) for *real* female friends. Not users and manipulators. Not jealous, petty, self-serving people, but godly women who would help bring me closer to God.

And God answered. Not long ago, my friend Sarah from Kentucky called to tell me she was taking a day to *fast* for me—to pray for God to work in my life. I'd never had a friend fast for me. What an incredible blessing! Now she wants to fix me up with someone who works in her office. We single women need female friends like that! Not only for their prayer support and encour-agement, but because there's a good chance that, through one of them, we'll meet the one God has for us. And when we do find that person, friends like this will still be around.

My friend Uri and I spent hours together praying during the

2000 presidential elections. Uri is a blast, and her counsel is right in line with the Word of God. When I got tickets to the Presidential Ball, she was one of the twenty I took with me. She's a radio host and carried her recorder around all night. She got interviews with Secretary of State Katherine Harris, Governor Jeb Bush, and most of the cabinet. When she stuck the microphone in my face and asked me how I felt, I told her I was going to celebrate by "dancing *all night long!*" Imagine my surprise when she aired that little clip on her extremely conservative radio station (they play hymns—not Steven Curtis Chapman) the next morning. (I should have followed my own advice, straight from the "Media" chapter in *True to Life*: "*Never* say anything you don't want on the air!")

Then there's my "Florida mom" Lil. I just got two cards from her. One says, "If He is God, He is still in charge." Inside, it says, "He is." And it has the words of Isaiah 45:5: "I am the LORD, and there is no other; apart from me there is no God. I will strengthen you...." I'm sharing this because I thought it would encourage you just as it did me. We all need a Lil in our lives—the kind of godly woman who is mentioned in Titus 2:3–5.

I met Guyla while speaking at a pro-life rally in Nebraska. She knows how hard it is to be on the front lines, especially when you're alone. She gave me Psalm 20 to read that day. It's marked in my Bible with the date 1/22/00: "May He grant you your heart's desire and fulfill all your counsel!... May the LORD fulfill all your petitions.... May the King answer us in the day we call" (vv. 4–5, 9, NASB). She is a prayer warrior and an encouraging friend.

And, remember, some of our close friends need to be single

so we have someone to go with to parties. Nothing's worse than walking into a place where you don't know many people—alone, feeling like there's a huge L (for Loser) on your forehead.

Pray for real friends, godly people whom you admire and want to be like. Then make an effort to find them—uplifting people you can laugh with as you grow closer to God.

AROUND THE CORNER

My friend Evan's mom gave me a wonderful perspective on one of my favorite people in the Bible, David. You know all those chapters where King Saul is jealous of him and is seeking his life? Those chapters when David is hiding in caves with his men? Well, a few pages of that and then David becomes king of Israel. Piece of cake. But you know what? *David* didn't know that was coming. He was in a cold, dark, damp cave with his men. They were all hungry and tired and fleeing for their lives. *They* didn't know what was going to happen in the next chapter. As far as they knew, around the corner they would face more of the same—or worse.

But David trusted God. He trusted God when he was in the caves. And God worked on David during those dark days. David learned to trust. That's when he wrote a lot of the psalms we now turn to when we're hurting.

David trusted God even when things were bleak. He waited on God, and God gave him enough to get through it. He gave David his friend Jonathan, faithful men, and unshakable faith in the goodness of God. "For I hear the slander of many; there is terror on every side; they conspire against me and plot to take my life. But I trust in you, O LORD; I say, 'You are my God.' My times are in your hands" (Psalm 31:13–15).

That's what we have to do. Even though our world seems cold, dark, and lonely, God is there. He's in control. He is *for* us. And He sees what's around the corner even when we can't. Remember, faith, like film, is developed in the dark. Trust was made for the darkness. We can count on every word He says—so we know He's working it all for our good. Turn the page. The next chapter of your life is going to be beyond what you can think or imagine (Ephesians 3:20).

One of David's kingly qualities was that he wouldn't manipulate events to his advantage. He could have easily killed Saul on more than one occasion. He even cut a piece of fabric from Saul's robe to prove it (1 Samuel 24:4). But he didn't take matters into his own hands and make himself king.

Now, I'm not advocating that we sit back and wait for God to do everything. David fought for his life. He volunteered to kill Goliath, after all, and God used him. And eventually made him king. He just didn't manipulate things to bring it about more quickly.

I think God blesses us with the one He wants us to have when we step out in faith—and volunteer to be used by Him. We must be willing to act—but not to manipulate. Keep trusting Him in the dark times, because He has something great for us in the next chapter—right around the corner!

NEW YEAR'S EVE

It's now 7:34 on New Year's Eve, and I'm sitting on a plane from Cleveland to Fort Lauderdale. I was supposed to be there a few days ago to see my boyfriend race. Yeah, he races and while he's been to hear a lot of my speeches, I've never seen him race. I know I run the risk of offending some of you, but I just can't believe how many people are into NASCAR. I'm sorry, but I just don't *get* it—three hours of watching cars circle around a track? I told my boyfriend this and, well, he didn't much care for my analysis. Maybe that's why we're no longer dating.

I got to him once, though. He came over but had to let himself in because I was sitting, in a trancelike state, in front of the TV with a NASCAR race blaring. I was on the edge of the couch, clutching the blanket, watching every turn. I'd never seen him so happy. He ran to me and asked me to marry him while I tried to look past his head at the race—waving him to be quiet so I wouldn't miss a single turn. He tried to kiss me—but I wouldn't let him block the screen!

Oh, the memories!

Well, I didn't go to his race, of course, because he dumped me. But before we broke up, he bought me a Christmas tree—and now I get to go home and take it down by myself. I hate the thought. I think I'll leave it up.

So, traveling alone on New Year's Eve, I went through airport security hoping not to see anyone. That's when I heard someone shouting my name and looked up to see a man running toward me.

It was my ex-boyfriend's coworker. *Lovely.* Not only am I alone on New Year's; now my ex is going to hear about it. Ever have one of those days?

Earlier that afternoon, I was looking at all the newly placed decorations at the local drugstore when my mother said, "Valentine's Day is just around the corner!" Thanks for the glad tidings, Mom. Can't *wait.*

The good news, I guess, is that I don't have a lot of happy New Year's memories to lament over. I can't remember many I really liked. So at least I'm not looking back longingly. There's a silver lining for you.

The flight attendant just served our airplane meal. What d'you know? New Year's Eve dinner. And the chicken in the sandwich is crunchy because it's still frozen. Otherwise, it tastes great. The girl next to me just bit into her frozen chocolate, and I think she lost a tooth. It's pretty cold in Cleveland.

Wanna hear something even more pathetic? This year's New Year's Eve is better than last year's. So, don't tell me I don't know what it's like. If this book doesn't help someone, *I'm going to be really mad.*

Yeah, I can focus on what must have been at least ten pounds I gained while at home. I actually purposely left behind homemade fudge to keep from finishing every last piece. (Here's another aside: You want to lose weight? Get that stuff out of your house, and don't bring in any more. It won't help the situation anyway. Handy tip, huh? Maybe that can be the topic of my next book.)

It's now 8:03 PM and I'm looking out the window. (Hey! I

could have been in a middle seat—that's something to be thankful for!) I see cars on the highways—people heading to their New Year's Eve parties—many of them, I'm thinking, without purpose in their lives. *At least they have a date.* But a lot of them are going out to drink in the New Year. There are all kinds of ways to deal with loneliness. We can turn to painkillers like alcohol or drugs—which will have side effects far worse than the problems we're trying to escape. Or turn to the One who can actually do something about the problems we face.

Here's the bottom line: You can feel miserable about your situation, or you can choose to believe that God is in control and that He has something for you to do right now. I pick the latter. I choose, unlike New Year's Eves past, to embrace what God has for me—even though I really don't care for it much.

Sometimes I even hate it. Like right now. But rather than focus on my feelings and circumstances, I'm going to focus on what I know is true: God is real, His Word is true, His way is best. He hears us and will answer when we call on Him. Let's:

> God, I thank You that You are a good God. I thank You that You are intimately involved in our lives; that You know the number of the hairs on our heads—a seemingly insignificant fact—but yet You have, for some reason, chosen to keep a record. I know that a sparrow doesn't fall to the ground without Your noticing, and so You, God, are aware of what is going on right now. And You care.
>
> You're the One who said that it is not good for man to

be alone. You are the One who promised to give us the desires of our hearts if we delight in You. You said you set the solitary in families. You bless those who fear You with a spouse "like a fruitful vine" and children like "olive plants" around their table. Lord, I would like to be blessed that way, and I'm praying that You will bless me like that *this coming year.*

I'm praying that prayer for my friends who are reading this. God, I know that You hear us. And if only one person reads this book, then we are two or more "gathered together" praying in Your name. We know that You are here with us, because You have told us so, and we know that every word You have spoken is true. *Every word.* We ask then, in faith, that You will not only hear us, but answer us as well.

Strengthen us and enable us to do Your will now so once we have done Your will, we know we will receive what You have promised us, the one that You have for us. Please make us ready quickly!

God, we also know that that prayer changes things. After all, You told Moses that You would do the very thing He asked because You were pleased with him and knew him by name. Well, if You know the hairs on our heads, then You know *us* by name. We are Your children through Your Son, Jesus. And if our earthly father would give us good things, how much more will You, our *heavenly* Father?

I also ask for safety on this very bumpy plane. And I ask Your forgiveness for complaining about being here. God, while I've been a whiny spoiled brat, I really am grateful for this life You have given me. I am glad to be alive, and I want to live to see the next year. New Year's Eve alone is far better than no New Year's at all. Thank You for life, dear God. Thank You for the breath You have given me today. I know that it is only in You that we live and breathe, and have our being.

Thank You for Your many, many blessings. I thank You that I live in America. I thank You for freedom. I thank You that, compared to most other countries, we live as royalty. Lord, help us to share what You have given us with others less fortunate. Help us to reach out to those near us with Your love, with the hope of salvation—the gift that You have provided for us at the ultimate cost. Break through the veils and blinders to reach those in our families and those we love—*this* year. God, we are here because of You. You have created us; You have made us in Your image. You have a plan for our lives—one that You have destined since the foundation of the world. God, I want that plan. I want that perfect plan You have for my life. I want to join You in what You are doing right here and now at this place in history where You have placed us. Lord, work through us to change it for good. God, I want my life to count—to make a God-sized impact on those around me, in my work, in this nation, and beyond.

Lord, we come humbly before You and submit to You. We surrender to You. We give You all of our hopes and dreams and expectations and ask You to replace them with Yours. We trust You, God. You are *for* us. And You have told us that You can do exceedingly abundantly more than we can think or imagine. I want greater things for my life than I can think or imagine. Your ways really are higher than our ways. Your thoughts really are greater than our thoughts. I thank You for that.

I thank You that not only can You conceive of better things than we could ever hope to, but that You are powerful enough to carry them out. God, please carry them out—and blow us away this year in every area of our lives! Please set things in motion for Your plan. I'm finished fighting for my way. I want Your way—but I want it now! Okay, I'll submit to Your timing too, but it's really, really hard, God. You control the circumstances, and that means that You control *when* they happen. So, while I submit to Your perfect plan, in Your perfect time, I'm also asking You to *please* hurry it up. If You can in any way hurry it up without messing everything up, I humbly ask You to do that.

Thank You for what You are going to do. Please give me the desires for things that are of You, God. Give me a hunger for Your Word, a hunger to spend time with You—every day. Lord, please also give me the desire for things that are good for me. Help me to take care of this temple You have given me. Thank You for giving me the ability to see and hear and walk. God, forgive me for taking these things for granted. Help me to do the things that will bring me into the center of Your perfect will in my spirit, my mind, and my body.

Please guard my thoughts, Lord, from the lies all around me. Lord, I choose to believe You. I love You, and I thank You that You are in control and the circumstances I am in now are for a purpose. Help me to fulfill that purpose. Help me to learn what You would have me to learn. And, God, please bring Your very best for me soon. Thank You, my Father. I can't wait to see what You have in store for me.

In the name of Your Son, the name above all names, the most powerful name in heaven and on earth—the name of Jesus Christ—I pray. Amen.

A long-winded prayer—I know. But I thought it a better use of book space than more of my ramblings. Pray—take your case to the God who can do something about your situation. Who can do *anything.*

And did you catch the bumpy ride in that prayer? Isn't it amazing what a little turbulence in an airplane can do for your attitude? Nothing like a brush with death to make you appreciate your life—something that didn't seem worth a whole lot just moments before.

THE TACKY PARTY

Since we're in the coffee shop, still finishing our chocolate cake, I thought this would be a good time to tell you about a party I went to in Cincinnati, *between* Christmas and New Year's one year, that was way more fun than any New Year's Eve I've ever had.

It was a theme party, and the theme was "tacky." I went with a guy I knew casually from church. On the drive down we stopped at a pay phone and called the host, to let him know "we're going to be late." We called collect, of course—remember the theme.

His answer set us up for what the night would be like: "That's okay. Only a half dozen people are here so far, so I'm still in my robe. I need to wait for a few more people before I take my shower."

We showed up with half a bottle of wine and most of a fruit basket—with the names on the card scratched out to make room for the host's. With the ambience of tacky Christmas music in the background, we had a blast asking people how old they were and how much money they made.

Our host was a riot. He *inspired* creativity. Apparently, at last year's event, he ate steak while everyone else was served pizza.

I told him I was cold and started looking around his house for something to wear. He followed me into his room to watch me go through his dresser drawers searching for a sweatshirt—acting as though this was a normal thing to do with someone you just met.

I came out to find my date asking a woman how much she weighed.

Having decided that I didn't care all that much for the food being served, I went to the kitchen and started rummaging through the refrigerator and cupboards. Finally I broke out the popcorn machine—since that made the biggest mess—and the rest of the party moved into the kitchen and joined in looking for vegetable oil, popcorn, and bowls.

As we amused ourselves, my date picked up our host's mail and started reading it out loud, with commentary on the interesting tidbits. "Late in paying your phone bill, huh? I hope there's not a problem there.... Those 976 numbers can really add up, huh?"

I'm not sure he ever had *another* tacky party, but I can tell you, that one was a blast! In fact, it inspired a similar party for my girlfriend Abby when she got engaged.

My friends and I dressed her up in a big white hoop skirt and gave her fiancé a loud plaid sports jacket and clip-on bow tie. We put them in the back of my convertible with a sign that read "JUST (about to be) MARRIED" and drove them to the local cafeteria—horns honking, of course. We took them to the cafeteria's "party room," where everyone was waiting as if it were the reception. The head table was decorated with paper wedding bells and those plastic Christmas candles complete with orange lightbulbs that people used to put in their windows (with one bulb unscrewed so it wouldn't light). The bride and groom, after standing in line for their food, fed each other a piece of lemon meringue pie, which came, naturally, with the plastic wedding-cake couple on top.

A buddy of mine was the deejay, and he played all the wedding classics—"The Hokey Pokey," "The Bunny Hop," and "The Electric Slide." He also insisted on some polka numbers. Another friend put on a long wig and Birkenstocks and pretended to be Abby's long-lost boyfriend, "Bobby." He grabbed the microphone and made a final plea for her "not to do it"—after all, he'd "just put *new carpet* in the van." Who *wouldn't* call off her wedding with an offer like that?

They hung the poster of pictures from that night at the real wedding reception. One of the guests was overheard telling another, "Yeah, that's her old boyfriend, Bobby. He tried to get her back."

So, finished your chocolate cake yet? What were we talking about? Oh, yeah. Breaking up...

Notes from My Journal

You've broken up. No matter who initiated it, no matter what the reason, it hurts. Sometimes it hurts so much you wonder how you're going to get through it. Sometimes it hurts so much that you don't even care if you do. It's a crippling, debilitating, oppressive pain that the light of day can't penetrate. To say what you're going through is "hard" is like saying what happened on September 11 was "bad." No matter what anyone says to you, no matter what they do, all you can feel is pain.

Only God can penetrate a heart that is *that* broken. God's words. God's hope. God's love.

The thing you *have* to remember is that your Father is a good Father. Think of a toddler who has to get a shot. He doesn't understand that he needs medicine to stay well. All he knows is that he's afraid of that big needle. So what does he do? He wraps his arms around his father's neck and holds on tight. Even if his dad lets the mean nurse stick him with the needle, he knows his father will comfort him. How does he know that? Because even when his dad allows the pain, the child *knows* he is a good dad. He knows his dad loves him. He has seen it all of his life. He knows his dad will care for him and help him through the pain—even when he doesn't understand it. And so he trusts him.

Remember the spiritual war we're in? Satan is putting lies in your mind right now about your heavenly Father, telling you that God doesn't care about you, that He has forgotten you. Satan first attacked the character of God in the Garden of Eden. Eve knew how good God was. She had everything and it *really was* perfect. But one doubt—one little arrow of doubt—made her wonder if maybe the God she trusted was holding out on her. Maybe He was holding back something good. Satan attacked Eve's confidence in God's kindness, in God's character. And she fell for it.

Don't fall for the same old trick Satan has been using since the Garden of Eden.

Go back to the first chapter and look again at what we talked about. God is good. He is for us. His plan is not to harm us, but to prosper us. His plan is for *our good*, to give us "hope and a future" (Jeremiah 29:11). He's a good Dad. You can cling to Him even when it hurts—especially when it hurts.

When you're hurting is when you most need to get alone with God and His Word and pour out your heart to Him. Tell Him exactly how you feel. He's big enough to handle it all—even the part where you're not too pleased with Him. If David was a man after God's own heart, and that's what he did, I think it's probably okay.

But you'll notice that even though David felt forgotten by God (as we sometimes do), even though he had sorrow in his heart and his enemy was triumphing, he still trusted in God's unfailing love—even enough to sing about it:

> How long, O LORD? Will you forget me forever? How long will you hide your face from me? How long must I wrestle with my thoughts and every day have sorrow in my heart? How long will my enemy triumph over me?... But I trust in your unfailing love; my heart rejoices in your salvation. I will sing to the LORD, for he has been good to me. (Psalm 13:1–2, 5–6)

David's "spirit fails" as he cries out to God to get him out of the pit and onto level ground:

> Answer me quickly, O LORD; my spirit fails. Do not hide your face from me or I will be like those who go down to the pit. Let the morning bring me word of your unfailing love, for I have put my trust in you. Show me the way I should go, for to you I lift up my soul. Rescue me from my enemies, O LORD, for I hide myself in you. Teach me

to do your will, for you are my God; may your good Spirit lead me on level ground. For your name's sake, O LORD, preserve my life; in your righteousness, bring me out of trouble. (143:7–11)

David knows that God is the one who can preserve his life and take him out of his trouble.

God can do that for you, too.

I've also learned that even when you are depressed, even when things are horrible, *you can still praise God:* "Why are you downcast, O my soul? Why so disturbed within me? Put your hope in God, *for I will yet praise him,* my Savior and my God" (Psalm 42:11).

Praise God in your pain. Thank Him that He is a good God—despite what you see and feel. God's Word is like a healing balm. Place His words on the wounds in your heart. Spread them where it hurts. Every word is true; every word is 100 percent effective. You'll feel relief immediately.

Our heavenly Father has promised that He is near to the broken-hearted and saves those whose spirits are crushed (Psalm 34:18). He not only comforts us; He heals with His love and grace (147:3). We can take refuge in Him (57:1), knowing that He has promised that His grace is sufficient for us and His power is made perfect through our weakness (2 Corinthians 12:9). He will quiet us with His love (Zephaniah 3:17) if only we will heed Him: "Be still, and know that I am God" (Psalm 46:10).

It is during times of intense pain that I find myself running to God the most. I have found Him to be true to His word—

when we draw near to Him, He draws near to us (James 4:8). I was hurting one night so badly that I couldn't sleep. I got up and went to the living room with my Bible. According to my journal, it was three in the morning. I was crying and searching God's Word for some answers. Here's what I found:

> Therefore the LORD *longs* to be gracious to you, and therefore He waits on high to have compassion on you. For the LORD is a God of justice; how blessed are all those who long for Him. O people in Zion, inhabitant in Jerusalem, *you will weep no longer. He will surely be gracious to you at the sound of your cry;* when He hears it, *He will answer you.* Although the Lord has given you bread of privation [adversity] and water of oppression, He, your Teacher will no longer hide Himself, but your eyes will behold your Teacher. Your ears will hear a word behind you, "This is the way, walk in it," whenever you turn to the right or to the left. (Isaiah 30:18–21, NASB)

God said He *longs* to be gracious to me. And though He was talking to Jerusalem in this passage, that night I felt Him talking to *me* when He said "you will weep no longer. He will surely be gracious to you at the sound of your cry; when He hears it, He will answer you." That was exactly what I needed to hear. I had been given what I felt was the "bread of [adversity] and water of oppression." And if God wasn't going to "hide Himself" from me any longer, then I couldn't wait.

In the midst of adversity, David wrote, "You have taken account of my wanderings; put my tears in Your bottle. Are they not in Your book?" (Psalm 56:8, NASB). Dutch Sheets, in his book *How to Pray for Lost Loved Ones*, suggests that the "bottle" isn't a storage container. The word used is *nodah*, which means a skin used to transform juice to wine, or cream to butter. When God is finished, they will be changed, says Sheets, "into wine—fruitfulness." They are to be used by God, not wasted—transformed into something else.[3]

Psalm 126:5–6 (NASB) says, "Those who sow in tears shall reap with joyful shouting. He who goes to and fro weeping, carrying his bag of seed, shall indeed come again with a shout of joy, bringing his sheaves with him." Sheets says that in this verse our tears are like seeds—seeds God uses to produce a fruitful harvest. If that's the case, I'm in a good place, because I feel as though I've given Him a lot of seeds to work with. You too?

God has a purpose for you, and He will fulfill it. He will send His love and faithfulness:

Have mercy on me, O God, have mercy on me, for in you my soul takes refuge. I will take refuge in the shadow of your wings until the disaster has passed. I cry out to God Most High, to God, who fulfills his purpose for me. He sends from heaven and saves me, rebuking those who hotly pursue me; God sends his love and his faithfulness. (Psalm 57:1–3)

God says that if we devote our hearts to Him and turn from our sin, we will forget our trouble, be secure, and find hope and rest.

Once I was afraid because of a noise I heard in the middle of the night. After fearfully checking all the doors and setting the burglar alarm, I was still too scared to sleep. I turned to my Bible and "just happened" to read this:

"You will be secure, because there is hope; you will look about you and take your rest in safety. You will lie down, with no one to make you afraid, and many will court your favor." (Job 11:18–19)

God reached down and told me that everything was going to be okay. I will lie down, with no one to make me afraid. I kind of like that "many will court my favor" bonus too.

Feel that you can't go on anymore? Paul felt that way too. But he cried out to the God who raises the dead, the God on whom he set his hope, the God who delivers us:

For we do not want you to be unaware, brethren, of our affliction which came to us in Asia, that we were burdened excessively, beyond our strength, so that we despaired even of life; indeed, we had the sentence of death within ourselves so that we would not trust in ourselves, but in God who raises the dead; who delivered us from so great a peril of death, and will deliver us, He on whom we have set our hope. *And He will yet deliver us.* (2 Corinthians 1:8–10, NASB)

These verses are especially meaningful to me. I read them during the 2000 elections and kept going back to them—again and again. If you're going to put your hope in someone, pick someone who can deliver. If He can raise the dead, He can deliver you. He has promised us: "Those who hope in me will not be disappointed" (Isaiah 49:23).

Use this breakup time to draw close to Him, and He will speak to you as He never has before. Let Him reach down to you and assure you that He's aware of what you're going through and has you safely in the palm of His hand. Trust in your God—let Him heal you and then let Him show you what He has for you around the corner.

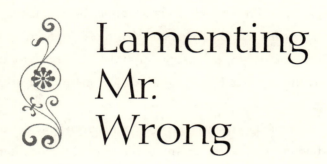

five

Lamenting Mr. Wrong

CLOSING THE DOOR ON THE PAST

Reading through this book, you may think I had dates every night. Or that I was always crying in hotel rooms. Neither is really true. I have dated a lot, but there have also been times—sometimes more than a year—when I wasn't really interested in dating anyone. One thing is clear though—I see just how much time I've wasted lamenting Mr. Wrong.

This is the issue I struggle with most. I once cried over a guy for a *full year*. Actually, I've done that more than once. But if you're like me, after a breakup you may also find yourself remembering all the good times and forgetting the reasons that led you apart.

The worst of it is that when God's blessings and perfect plan are right in front of your face, Satan is going to distract you and have you looking back so that you don't see them. And don't forget what happened to Lot's wife when she looked back!

That's why closed doors are actually better than a lot of doors left partway open. I've always left all the options open, thinking it was in my best interest. But I've found that those "options" have been what kept me from looking forward. I've turned to ex-boyfriends the moment I felt low, which just means more time wasted on a guy who's not the right one for me.

If you're looking back, whether the door is open wide or only a crack, find out if it's right or wrong. Either walk through it, or shut it and move on. We need to recognize that guys who string us along are actually closed doors, no matter how wide open they seem. Proverbs 27:5 states it this way: "Better is open rebuke than hidden love."

A good friend (and ex-boyfriend) recently came for a visit. We had a blast together—just like old times. The next thing I knew he was sending me extravagant presents in the mail and writing me letters about how wonderful I was and how his time with me was "life changing." My friends told me, "This guy is in love with you." But I had already spent far too much of my life lamenting him. I didn't want to waste another minute hoping that the cracked door would swing open.

So I asked him. Straight out.

Nope. He wasn't looking to rekindle anything—just acting like it. I'm glad I know. I'll take open rebuke over hidden love any day. Now I can keep looking forward.

The problem is that once you give your heart away, you can't get it back. My friend Mickey told me bluntly, "Jan, you gave your heart away, and this guy stored it in his garage."

A guy may *tell* you that you're the love of his life, but actions are what's real. So I've decided, after wasting years regretting guys who had my heart stored in their garage instead of displayed on their mantel as a cherished part of their life, that I'm going to give my heart to God for safekeeping. No one's going to get it until He says so. And he's going to have to go to God for it.

I just told a guy who is pursuing me, "If you want to get close to me, get close to God." I don't want anyone who's not. And He's the One who is keeping watch over my heart.

My track record on picking the right guy isn't all that swift, so I don't want to do the choosing anymore. It may be that the "life of the party" isn't my best match. It may be that someone who is "exactly like me" won't provide anything I'm missing. I want God's choice. He knows every heart. He knows the future, and He knows what I need.

He knows what each one of us needs.

My prayer is that God will change my heart to match His selection. And the guy He has for me is not *ever* going to leave me wondering. If he's the one for me, he's going to do the pursuing— and leave no doubts about his feelings or intentions.

Your heart is incredibly precious. In fact, it's priceless. So close the door. Get your heart back. And give it to God for safe-keeping.

And then there's all the second-guessing about how you handled things.

I don't know why, but when you're the one ending the relationship, it's that much harder. Did you do the right thing? Should you have given it another chance? My last boyfriend broke up with me. It was because I was struggling with his divorce and his past, but *he* was the one who ended it. Somehow that's easier. You don't have to second-guess the breakup. You can put it all in God's hands and let Him handle it. He may have allowed the breakup for a reason—like for me to finish writing a book, for example.

Remember that our lives are in the hands of an all-powerful God—who is intricately involved in the plan for *all* of our days. That means He's involved in what happens today. And what happened yesterday. We are not in the hands of blind chance, but of a purposeful and deliberate God. And sometimes He moves people out of our lives for our own good. It's His design we want, after all—not ours. We need to stop worrying and rest in that. God has it all under control, and He wants what's best for us.

But maybe it wasn't the guy who blew the relationship. Maybe it was *you*. I think this is worse. Not only are things miserable; they're miserable because of you. That may mean that you can fix them. But you have to remember that God is still in control. This is a time to be in serious prayer—because it could also be that the situation isn't *supposed* to be fixed. My big fear is that I could mess up something God has for me. But if I seek Him and walk where

He leads me, I'm sure He can fix things even when I mess up.

This verse really helped me when I thought I had messed up "the" relationship God had planned for me: "I know that you can do all things; no plan of yours can be thwarted" (Job 42:2). God is God and He can do whatever He wants. He has a plan for each of our lives—which means even *we* can't thwart it.

Maybe we can reject God and His perfect plan for our lives. People throw away their marriages every day despite the fact that God hates divorce. They kill children even though God hates the shedding of innocent blood. When we disobey God, we bear the consequences and the pain that come with that disobedience.

But what if we're seeking God and submitting to Him? What if we want what God wants, and we obey Him? If the Lord orders our steps, it seems to me that He will take us where He wants us, even if we mess up along the way by taking some wrong turns. I believe He can guide us back when we take a wrong turn. If God wants us to be with that certain person and if we submit to Him, He can make it so.

I spent a miserable year wondering if I had blown it with my former fiancé. Was he really God's best for me? I submitted to God and asked Him—repeatedly—for His best. Whatever that might be. During that time, I got closer to God. And He gave me another chance with my ex. But at the same time my boyfriend grew further from God. He told me he was mad at God because things didn't work out—and he turned away from Him. He told me he wasn't the same person. And he was right. You know what? I don't want someone who turns away from

God when the bottom drops out. That's when we need Him more than ever—especially in marriage.

In Acts 5, when the religious leaders were trying to stop Peter and the other apostles from preaching the gospel and healing, a Pharisee named Gamaliel said, "Therefore, in the present case I advise you: Leave these men alone! Let them go! For if their purpose or activity is of human origin, it will fail. *But if it is from God, you will not be able to stop these men*; you will only find yourselves fighting against God" (vv. 38–39). This seems to suggest that, if the relationship is from God, then you won't be able to stop it. Submit to His plan and it won't be thwarted.

God has His way even in things as mundane as a coin toss or drawing lots: "The lot is cast into the lap, but its every decision is from the LORD" (Proverbs 16:33). After you've prayed about an issue, and done all you can do to fix it, quit worrying: "Do not be anxious about anything, but in everything, by prayer and petition, with thanksgiving, present your requests to God" (Philippians 4:6); "Cast all your anxiety on him because he cares for you" (1 Peter 5:7).

A GOD'S-EYE VIEW

Remember Joseph? Coat of many colors, sold into slavery, thrown into prison.... He had it pretty miserable there. Yet all that time he was in the center of God's will. He had to be sold into slavery to meet Potiphar; he had to be falsely accused of rape by Potiphar's wife so he could be thrown into prison; he had to get thrown into prison so he could meet Pharaoh's cupbearer; he had to meet the cupbearer so he could interpret his dream; he had to interpret his dream so Pharaoh could hear about him. That was when Joseph told the cupbearer, "But when all goes well with you, remember me and show me kindness; mention me to Pharaoh and get me out of this prison" (Genesis 40:14).

But the cupbearer forgot him. *Jerk.*

For two lousy, stinkin' years, Joseph was in that prison. Yet he was in the center of God's will. He hadn't done anything wrong (although telling his brothers about his dreams where they all bowed to him wasn't too bright), and yet he sat in jail for two more years.

A bit of good news—he got favor from the prison warden, and the Lord gave him success in everything he did (Genesis 39:21–23). But why couldn't God tell the stupid cupbearer to remember sooner? Well, think about it for a minute. "Hey, Pharaoh, I met this neat guy in prison, where you sent me, who can interpret dreams—cool, huh? We could use a guy like that around here. What do you say we let him out?" Yeah, *that* would have gone over well. Maybe it's just me, but it seems Pharaoh was a pretty touchy guy—and if you caught him in the wrong mood, well, you might end up like his baker—beheaded and hanging from a tree.

The fact is, Joseph wasn't relevant information until Pharaoh had a strange dream. *That's* when the cupbearer tells him about his prison buddy. Why couldn't God give Pharaoh the dream faster? Yeah, I've asked that one too. God must have needed to prepare Joseph for all He had for him to do.

But Joseph didn't know that. He was sitting in prison after a string of some seemingly less-than-fortunate events—like being sold into slavery. Yet it was God's will. I can't imagine it seemed like it to Joseph, but that's exactly where God had to put Joseph so he could meet Pharaoh, interpret his dream, save the country and his family from starvation, and be reconciled with them all.

I've been involved in the political arena for years now, and I can tell you it takes a lot of years and a lot of connections to work your way up the ladder to be the number two guy in the country—which is what Joseph became. God's plan was probably the most time-efficient one too! I think the important thing was that God formed Joseph during those years. Joseph continued to trust in God even though he had no earthly reason to.

God sees the whole picture. You're where you are for a reason. God is working things for your good, so trust Him, even if you hate it. Even if it's taking too stinkin' long! Joseph did—and God came through. He will do it for you too—in His way and in His time. And while it's better to be single wishing you were married than married wishing you were single, being content (and grateful) where God has you is best of all.

As you may have guessed, timing is perhaps the thing I struggle with most. Joseph probably didn't care for it much either. But God had a plan—even if Joseph couldn't see it. The same is true for us. "The Lord is not slow in keeping his promise, as some understand slowness" (2 Peter 3:9). Although I think *I* understand slowness—and this wait sure seems slow to me, considering what God can do in a week. Look outside for a minute. See the trees? The sky? Hills, mountains, rivers, oceans, birds? God created everything in less than a week. Seems we shouldn't have to wait longer than that for something much simpler.

Good thing God's thoughts and ways are higher than ours. Otherwise I would have lost hope by now. He *will* work things out for our good. That's the one sure thing, and if God wants me to write a book to encourage singles to start living for Him instead of watching the clock and lamenting how they haven't found Mr. Right, then that's just what I want to do. I don't want to be even an inch out of the center of God's will—even though it's not always the easiest place to be.

Okay, I need to make a confession. After I got off the plane New Year's Eve, I ended up going to one of those parties. And it wasn't boring. After playing some games, we prayed in the New Year. I'm glad I went. After all my whining about being alone on New Year's Eve and being so "spiritual" that I was going to stay home and write...well, *I didn't*. Laughing with my friends was way better than pouting at home—even if it doesn't make for a sacrificial, superspiritual story line.

RESISTING THE QUICK FIX

Before I left Florida at Christmas, I got a call from a guy I know who wanted to get together. He is cute and a lot of fun—but I know he isn't the right guy for me. A danger I face is that, if he asks me out again, I'm going to have a really hard time saying no since the "I'm leaving town" excuse will be gone. The next time will be harder still—and I might end up wasting a lot of time with a great guy that I know I can't marry. Even knowing this, I still struggle with it—just like you. It *is* more fun going out than sitting at home. But our God is the God of long-term happiness and joy, which is better than short-term fun—even if it doesn't seem like it at the time.

Satan's specialty is the quick fix. Though I don't know what it's like to be tempted by drugs, I know that people take them for a high—to feel good for a short time. But keep turning to that quick fix and it will destroy you. That's Satan's ultimate plan. That's what he uses to tempt married people into committing adultery. And many fall for it—they break their vows, destroy their marriages, and leave their children with the heartbreaking aftermath—all for a little short-term fun. What a rip-off. Compare that to married couples who have weathered the storms—whose families are intact. Trade in God's long-term plan for short-term fun? What a stupid idea. Yet people fall for it every day.

It's kind of like final exams in college. You can study or go out with your friends. If going out means failing your finals, I'm guessing no amount of fun will be worth it. It's just hard to see when you're faced with the choice. Short term all you can see is that studying isn't fun; going out is. But from the long term, flunking out of school isn't fun; graduating is. Hard to believe, but *a lot* of people stumble because they can't see the big picture.

That's the difference between Satan's plan and God's plan. Satan would encourage you to buy everything your heart desires on your credit card. Does that mean Satan is for you? Uh, no. While he may tempt you with short-term fun, he knows bills are coming that you can't pay. God, like any good parent, looks beyond the moment to your ultimate happiness. What good is your brand-new big-screen TV (that you really, *really* wanted) if you can't pay the rent or mortgage on your house? Which would you rather have: short-term fun or long-term happiness?

My friend Sarah came into my office one day and told me what a rough time she was having being single. She said she knew she could come to me because I understand. I guess it's great to be an expert in something. She, too, had a nice guy pursuing her, but she didn't really see much of a future. But why *shouldn't* they go out? He was a really great guy. I gave her my advice and predicted what would happen on a series of Post-it notes spread across my desk.

"Here's the deal," I said. "You hang out with this guy, you're going to start liking each other more. That's what spending enormous amounts of time with someone generally does. That's why they tell married people not to hang out with people of the opposite sex. Contrary to popular belief, *time*, not absence, makes the heart grow fonder."

So here's how the Post-it note trail went: You start dating him, and you start liking him more. Two notes pictured a happy stick-figure couple at dinner, hand in hand, all smiles. But the problems—things that didn't bother you much to begin with— start to bother you more. Not so happy now. And if you can't live with them, then (the Post-it notes fanned out into different directions) you're going to have to split, causing pain, ruining the friendship, and making running into him awkward—which is far worse than where you started.

Sarah acknowledged all of that—but she still wanted to see him. I totally understood. I've done the same thing: the two happy Post-it note trade-off for a whole stack of sad ones. Last week Sarah called to tell me the Post-it note trail had just ended—exactly where I said it would. But not before her quiet time with God dried up, her journaling became almost nothing, and most of her prayers now related to "the guy." She not only fell for Mr. Wrong; she let him take the place of God. Just as most of us have.

She's getting back on track with God, but she'll have to watch for the trap, the common pitfall that seems almost impossible to resist—seeing the guy again. She just told me she's going out with him tonight. Could've predicted it. Done it many times myself. When you're feeling sad and lonely, those memories of laughing and fun will be more tempting than a piece of chocolate cake. That's when we need to draw near to God, to remember that we want His long-term happiness, not just fun in the short term.

If you're here right now, this is the time to remind yourself that you want God's best, and though He seems to be taking His good old time bringing it, trust Him. Trust His timing. Like Joseph and David, you can't see what God has for you around the corner. Use this time to get into His Word, to pray, to thank Him for having everything under control and for working it together for your good. He will see you through the lonely times.

The Bike

When you find yourself clinging to thoughts of Mr. Wrong, I want you to think of the bike. Evan's sister, Stephanie, related the concept to me this way: There was a little girl who didn't have a bicycle. She went to a garage sale down the street with her dad one day and saw a bike for sale. Just ten dollars! Unbelievable! No one sells a bike for ten dollars! Of course it was a bit rusty, and the handlebars were bent. The kickstand didn't work—but you don't really need a kickstand. And the back tire needed air—but that's easy enough to remedy. After all, it was only *ten dollars!* There could be *no reason* why her father wouldn't pay ten dollars for a bike for her. Her birthday was just two weeks away, and she wanted *that* bike!

Her dad said no.

How could he deny her this one little thing? How could he say no to the desire of her heart—especially since it was almost free?

What she didn't know was that her father already had a shiny new bike with a big red bow on it underneath a blanket in the garage—her birthday gift.

All the little girl could see was that this wasn't fair. "Yeah, my dad *says* he loves me, but then why wouldn't he give me this one thing that I want—the one thing that would make me happy?" So for the next two weeks she walked to school while all her friends flew by on their bikes, handlebar streamers and hair blowing in the breeze. They chinged their little bells as they rode by. Yes, it seemed that everyone was happy except her. Everyone had a bike except her. And it was a very, very long two weeks.

Her choice? She could throw a temper tantrum for two weeks and tell her dad just how unfair he was. She could question his love for her. Or, after pleading her case, she could trust him and remind herself that she had a good dad who loved her and had done a lot for her in the past. She could quit walking by the garage-sale house every day, longing for the one thing she didn't have, and start focusing on what she did have. Playing softball at the playground, for example. Once she got into the game, suddenly her life wouldn't be all about whether she had a bike.

When her focus was elsewhere, the two weeks passed much faster, and it was soon time for her loving father to unveil the shiny new bicycle with the streamers and the shiny bell and a blue and white basket on the front. The kickstand actually worked! And the handlebars were straight and strong and just the right height for her.

This is what our loving heavenly Father wants for us. Not the garage-sale special. While we're whining about a rusty old second-hand bike, God has something way better for us. We need to trust what He has in store for us.

It all comes down to faith. Remember the woman who touched Jesus' cloak and was healed? Why was she healed? Jesus said: "Daughter, *your faith* has healed you. Go in peace and be freed from your suffering" (Mark 5:34).

When the centurion came to Jesus asking Him to heal his servant, he didn't have any doubt. You remember—Jesus told the centurion that He would "go and heal him" (Matthew 8:7). But Jesus didn't need to go there to get the job done: "The centurion replied, 'Lord, I do not deserve to have you come under my roof. But *just say the word,* and my servant will be healed'" (v. 8). Jesus replied, "'I have not found anyone in Israel with such great faith.... Go! It will be done just as you believed it would.' And his servant was healed at that very hour" (vv. 10, 13).

I want faith like that so I can see God move in the same way!

God works through our faith. For some reason, that's how this whole deal is set up. Think about what happened in Nazareth. The people there knew Jesus as "the carpenter," as "Mary's son and the brother of James, Joseph, Judas and Simon." "Aren't his sisters here with us?" they wondered. "And they took offense at him" (Mark 6:3).

Jesus responded, "Only in his hometown, among his relatives and in his own house is a prophet without honor" (v. 4). It appeared that the locals didn't trust Jesus because they felt He was just one of "Mary's kids" from down the block. But watch what comes next: "He could not do any miracles there, except lay his hands on a few sick people and heal them. And he was amazed at their lack of faith" (vv. 5–6). Did you catch that? Jesus *could not* do any miracles there. Hey, if God can do all things, how can that be? I believe that God has chosen to work through people's faith. If you trust Him, the way the woman who touched His cloak did, and the way the centurion did, you will see God's power released. However, if you don't have faith, you may end up like the people of Nazareth—missing out. That's how important faith is. In fact, "It is impossible to please God" without it (Hebrews 11:6).

THE MINORITY REPORT

Remember Joshua and Caleb? They were two of the scouts sent to explore Canaan to see if Israel would be able to take it. All the other scouts reported that the land was very good (it took two men to carry a single cluster of grapes), but the people there were like giants: "We seemed like grasshoppers in our own eyes, and we looked the same to them" (Numbers 13:33). But the minority report trusted God: "If the LORD is pleased with us, he will lead us into that land, a land flowing with milk and honey, and will give it to us. Only do not rebel against the LORD. And do not be afraid of the people of the land, because we will swallow them up. Their protection is gone, but the LORD is with us. Do not be afraid of them" (14:8–9). The giants we face may make us look like grasshoppers, but the God we serve makes them look like grasshoppers.

What was God's reaction to the spies without faith? "Your children will be shepherds here for forty years, suffering for your unfaithfulness, until the last of your bodies lies in the desert" (14:33). Ouch. Then it got *worse.* "These men responsible for spreading the bad report about the land were struck down and died of a plague before the LORD" (v. 37). God doesn't look too favorably on those who don't trust in Him.

Look at how God views a lack of faith: "The LORD said to Moses, 'How long will these people *treat me with contempt?* How long will they refuse to believe in me, in spite of all the miraculous signs I have performed among them?'" (14:11). Our tendency would be to say, "Aw, they were just scared of the giants. That's not so bad. Conquering giants *is* scary." But that wasn't how God viewed it. God viewed a lack of faith as treating Him with contempt. Not something we want to be doing.

Yes, the circumstances were compelling; their fear was real. But if you'll remember from the beginning of the book, the truth is not dependent upon our feelings or our circumstances. What God says is the truth. Ever heard anyone tell you to "face reality"? Guess what? Reality isn't found in circumstances or in feelings: Reality is the Word of God. And trusting God is not a suggestion; it's a command.

In fact, the Bible suggests that if you don't have faith, you can forget about receiving anything from the Lord: "But when he asks, he must believe and not doubt, because he who doubts is like a wave of the sea, blown and tossed by the wind. *That man should not think he will receive anything from the Lord*; he is a double-minded man, unstable in all he does" (James 1:6–8). Wow. If you doubt, don't even think you'll receive *anything* from the Lord—that's a pretty serious penalty.

See where I'm going with this? Unless you want to be unstable in all you do, you must trust God with your life.

Trust Him

✱ But the Lord said to Moses and Aaron, "Because you did not trust in me enough to honor me as holy in the sight of the Israelites, you will not bring this community into the land I give them." (Numbers 20:12)

* "Is not my house right with God? Has he not made with me an everlasting covenant, arranged and secured in every part? Will he not bring to fruition my salvation and grant me my every desire?" (2 Samuel 23:5)

* As for God, his way is perfect; the word of the LORD is flawless.... It is God who arms me with strength and makes my way perfect. (Psalm 18:30,32)

* Some trust in chariots and some in horses, but we trust in the name of the LORD our God. (Psalm 20:7)

* But as for me, I trust in you. (Psalm 55:23)

* And when Daniel was lifted from the den, no wound was found on him, because he had trusted in his God. (Daniel 6:23)

* "And why do you worry about clothes? See how the lilies of the field grow. They do not labor or spin. Yet I tell you that not even Solomon in all his splendor was dressed like one of these. If that is how God clothes the grass of the field, which is here today and tomorrow is thrown into the fire, will he not much more clothe you, O you of little faith?" (Matthew 6:28–30)

* Now faith is being sure of what we hope for and certain of what we do not see. (Hebrews 11:1)

GOD KNOWS

Following one of the big breakups, I was not easily consoled. He was "the one," but we just couldn't make it work. I did the breaking up, but I was devastated. I remember crying out to God by my bedside, "I'm never going to find anyone as perfect for me as him!" And it struck a memory. I had said almost those *identical words* when I didn't get the job I wanted taking Ralph Reed's place as executive director of the Christian Coalition.

I had prayed a very similar prayer afterward. The job was exactly what I had been training for. It would have allowed me to make a difference on the issues that matter most to me—to help change the direction of our nation for good—and it was in Virginia Beach (I've always loved the ocean). This was *perfect*—because it would allow me to do all the things I wanted to do *and* be near the beach. Every other job even in the same *category* was located in Washington, D.C., or somewhere pretty far inland.

Here's the great news—God knows things we don't! He knew about the Center for Reclaiming America, and He led me there. I was the national director for five years. It gave me an opportunity to use my abilities to help reform our culture—exactly what I wanted to do. And it was in *Fort Lauderdale!* People pay *money* to go there every winter—and I got to *live* there. My office was less than two miles from the beach. Not a bad deal.

God knew where He wanted me—in a place I'd never heard of—but that's where the all-knowing part really comes into play.

So when I'm feeling despair—feeling that I would never find anyone as perfect for me as this guy—I remember that I thought the very same thing about the job. God knows people we don't. And even though we may have never met anyone we want to spend the rest of our lives with, He *knows* them. He knows what they do, where they live—even their phone numbers. And though it seems He could cut through a whole lot of red tape if He'd just pass that information along, I think He wants us to know that we can trust Him even when we can't see it. Before we get our new bike, our new job, or our new man, we can trust Him. He wants what's best for us, and He's powerful enough to pull it off.

The great heroes of the Bible were ordinary people. They had to learn to trust God too. Think of the apostles. Great men—all but one. Yet they couldn't see the big picture—and made some seemingly stupid blunders. They were with Jesus night and day and saw firsthand all the amazing things He could do—healing the sick, raising the dead, giving sight to the blind. One day they witnessed Jesus feeding five thousand people with a couple of fish and a few loaves of bread. These apostles picked up twelve baskets of leftovers. Then, in the *very next chapter,* they were faced with how to go about feeding *four thousand* people. They actually had *more food* and *fewer people* than a chapter before, but were dumbfounded about what to do.

Duh.

I don't think the apostles were stupid. I think they were just like us—human. And human beings have a hard time remembering important things when we're in a crisis. We can even lose sight of the fact that we have God with us—the God who recently rescued us from a very similar situation. God is so incredibly patient. I would've grabbed a megaphone from heaven for the people in Matthew 15: "*Remember* people! Remember twelve baskets of leftovers? *Where* did they come from? That's right. And *who* is still with you?"

So remember who you're dealing with—the God of the universe who has helped you before, through a situation probably *worse* than what you're facing right now.

Get a notebook and make a list of all the miraculous things you've seen God do. Keep adding to it. When *you're* facing four thousand hungry people, open it up and remember what God did for you in the last chapter.

Remember

* "In days to come, when your son asks you, 'What does this mean?' say to him, 'With a mighty hand the Lord brought us out of Egypt, out of the land of slavery.'" (Exodus 13:14)

* "Go over before the ark of the Lord your God into the middle of the Jordan. Each of you is to take up a stone on his shoulder...to serve as a sign among you. In the future, when your children ask you, 'What do these stones mean?' tell them that the flow of the Jordan was cut off before the ark of the covenant of the Lord. When it crossed the Jordan, the waters of the Jordan were cut off. These stones are to be a memorial to the people of Israel forever." (Joshua 4:5–7)

* "The Lord who delivered me from the paw of the lion and the paw of the bear will deliver me from the hand of this Philistine." (I Samuel 17:37)

* They confronted me in the day of my disaster, but the LORD was my support. He brought me out into a spacious place; he rescued me because he delighted in me. (Psalm 18:18–19)

* The things you planned for us no one can recount to you; were I to speak and tell of them, they would be too many to declare. (Psalm 40:5)

EL PASO

Before I leave this section, let me tell you about another time and place documented in my journal—El Paso, Texas—and how I learned that God wants to use us.

I was speaking at a women's luncheon in El Paso, to an audience of over a thousand. I wasn't in top form and did what I considered a pretty mediocre job. But my hosts were incredibly nice. When I was finished, I wanted to collapse in my room and rest until I flew out the next morning. But they were helping put on a crusade for kids in the area and invited me to come along. I tried to beg off, but they wouldn't hear of it.

I remember waiting in the hotel lobby for them to pick me up—not wanting to be there. When they were five minutes late, I decided that I was going to give them just ten more minutes before heading back up to my room. Really generous of me—especially for a girl who's always late. But they came about forty-five seconds before my arbitrary deadline, and I was stuck.

Well, we sat in the convention center loge at the top of the stadium-style bleachers—these people were bigwigs, after all. When the speaker asked for a show of hands from those who would like to turn their lives over to Jesus, I saw a girl's arm go up in the row just in front of me. I'm normally not that observant, but I also noticed that when the speaker asked those who had raised their hands to come forward, that girl spoke to the person with her and didn't go.

I felt a strong urge to go to that girl. I'd never felt anything like it before. I didn't say a word to anyone; I just slipped away. I walked around to the front of the auditorium and climbed up the bleachers to the very last row. I went through that row—"excuse me, excuse me, excuse me"—until I got to her. I asked her if she had given her life to Jesus and she told me she had.

I told her that I knew it was *tough* to go forward—I had done it myself—but it was important. I told her that I would go with her. She talked to her friend (a cousin), and they decided that they would both go forward to accept Christ as their Savior! So we walked down together, and I found a counselor for them to pray with. Leaving them in good hands, I started to walk back.

But the story doesn't end there. Turns out, a lady close to where I had been sitting worked at one of the radio stations owned by my host. My friends said hello to her, and she blurted out, "The most *amazing* thing just happened! You're not going to believe it! I've been praying for my niece to come to the Lord *for years* and nothing happens—until *this lady* comes out of nowhere and walks forward with her!" She couldn't contain her joy.

Sometimes God lets us see a glimpse of what He's doing

through us, to encourage us and keep us going. They may have flown me in for a speech, but I'm convinced that's not the reason I was in El Paso that day. I wrote down the events because I always want to remember what kind of God we have. A powerful God. A God who works through people. People like us.

CALMING THE STORM

While it's important that we remember what God has done for us, don't forget that He's capable of doing things we've *never* seen Him do. We can make the mistake of putting Him in a box—thinking that He works in only one way or in only one area.

Here's the verse that hangs inside my medicine cabinet so that I see it every day: "Behold, I am the LORD, the God of all flesh: is there *any thing too hard for me?*" (Jeremiah 32:27, KJV). I don't think anything is too hard for Him, yet somehow, I *often* think so. Know what I mean? I think the apostles did too.

Matthew 8 tells about when the apostles were out in the boat and this "furious storm" kicked up (v. 24). Waves were sweeping over the boat. It must have been bad, because even these seasoned fishermen thought they were going to die. Jesus wasn't worried. He was sleeping. The apostles ran to Him and said, "'Lord, save us! We're going to drown!'" (v. 25). Jesus rebuked the winds and the waves, and everything went completely calm. At this point, they "were terrified and asked each other, 'Who is this? Even the wind and the waves obey him!'" (Mark 4:41). Well, they should have had *some* idea. In the same chapter (Matthew 8) they had seen Jesus heal the leper, the centurion's servant, and Peter's mother-in-law.

But they hadn't seen Him calm a storm. So they did what we do—what *I* do, anyway. Somehow it's easy to believe that God can do what I've seen Him do before (that is, if I remember it). But for God to work in a whole new dimension seems much more difficult to grasp. Unless you remember that you're dealing with God. "Behold, I am the LORD, the God of all flesh: is there *any thing* too hard for me?"

Uh, *no*.

I've seen God do miraculous things in my work. "Impossible" victories—legislatively, politically, and in ministry. Yet I haven't seen Him as directly involved for me, personally. That doesn't mean He's not. It just means I haven't *seen* His involvement as much. And just because you haven't seen Him working as mightily in your personal life, it doesn't mean He isn't or *can't*. Here's the deal: God is "the same yesterday, today and forever," right? The God who created the earth and the galaxies in a week can find you a husband.

And if a sparrow doesn't fall to the ground without God's notice, don't you think He cares about you and your well-being? You're quite a bit more valuable to God than a bird. As far as we know, He didn't die on the cross for birds.

I've spent some time thinking about it, and you know what? God *has been* working pretty miraculously in my personal life. And a lot of the incredible things I've seen Him do have to do with timing. When I look back, I see His hand not only in my work, but in my personal life as well. While I always choose on the basis of what I want to happen *right now*, God has access to *all* the information, like the knowledge that if I would only wait a few months, my perfect house would be available—a house *I* didn't even know existed. And if I waited just a little longer, the three bills I was working on in the legislature would come up for a vote—on my *very last day* at Ohio Right to Life. Three pro-life bills passing the Ohio House of Representatives—kind of a nice going-away present, don't you think? I couldn't have planned that. But God did.

He guides our steps and directs our paths because He knows where we're going even when we don't. He is orchestrating it all behind the scenes, like a movie director who has already read the entire script—or, more like a director who has *written* the script. Even though you haven't read it yet, you can trust Him to pull it all together—at the perfect time.

You may have noticed that I struggle with trusting God's timing. But when I remember, when I *look back*, I can see that if I had rushed things, it never would have worked out as perfectly. God knows the desires of our hearts, and He knows the best way to fulfill them. If you struggle with this too, join me in saying it out loud: "I trust His timing." You *really* can.

Don't put God in a box. He is God, and with Him, *all things* are possible. *All things!* That includes calming the storm—and providing you with the one He has for you.

By the way, I just got a call from my mother. She's in Russia with Operation Christmas Child—giving out presents to poor children in Russian orphanages and telling them about Jesus. She and her day care put together over twelve hundred shoe boxes full of toys and gifts for children who won't get any other presents this year. My mom *rocks*. Anyway, she called to tell me that she found my husband over there. The search, apparently, is over (I should tell you, she was convinced I should marry the *last* one). I thanked her and told her I could concentrate fully on my book now.

My mother is the best encourager I have ever met, heard of, or read about. She has given me more world-changing pep talks than anyone. Without her, I would have given up a thousand times before getting where I am. If awards were given out in life, she would get Most Valuable Player.

My friend Tony has a really amazing mom too. He told me that whenever he faced a "Goliath" while growing up, his mother used to tell him, "In *this* house, *we slay giants!*" If you have a mom like this, get on your knees and thank God. I do.

My mom, who just *had* to remind me at New Year's that Valentine's Day was "just around the corner," told me of her new project: Operation Valentine. She's sending valentines to nursing homes. Sure, you can whine about not getting any valentines this year, or you can use your energy to give them to people who've been forgotten all year-round—not just on Valentine's Day. *God* hasn't forgotten them, but many people have. Nursing homes are filled with lonely people longing for a visitor. They long for someone—anyone—to reach out to them and let them know they are loved. You can do that.

The children at my mom's Christian day care are cutting out hearts right now. Getting out the red glitter. Letting those people know they're loved. It's still January, and my mom has already sent me two valentines—plus a whole stack of "made" ones for my ninety-four-year-old friend Greta. *That's* the kind of mom I have.

You can do that for someone else.

At last count, my mom is going to be the valentine supplier for *five* nursing homes and one hospital. Then she got two other day cares to each sponsor a nursing home. I told you my mom rocks. She just got a call from a mother whose child was having a sleepover who said, "I want you to know we're all making valentines and we're going to bring them in to you!" My mom inspires all those around her. In total, she brightened *seven* nursing homes and a hospital. I hope to be like her one day.

We need to take our eyes off ourselves and our situation, and obey God. Remember what He has done before, and remember that He can do things you've never seen Him do. He knows the person He has for you, and you can trust His timing. Just get ready and get active.

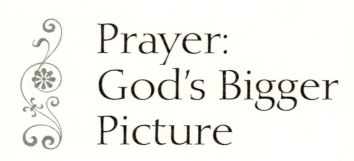 Prayer: God's Bigger Picture

A lot of people think that because I'm out there speaking and doing interviews that I have all kinds of opportunities to meet interesting people all the time. Surely at one of these events, I'll find *the one* who is the answer to all my prayers. Or he'll find me. After a national radio interview one day I got an interesting piece of fan mail. Here was a guy proposing to me by letter. Hang on—it gets better. He wrote, "Imagine me getting down on one knee asking for your hand in holy matrimony...because I'm looking for a woman *who can get me out of jail.*" That's right. Apparently he thought I was a lawyer and thus his perfect match.

I came into the office the next day and there was a picture of a wedding gown ripped out of some bridal magazine on my desk—

only this dress was completely covered with black stripes. My buddy Jeff sent me encouraging e-mails about how my "fiancé's friends could *steal* me some lovely wedding gifts." I, of course, let my parents in on the wonderful news and told them how I had been proposed to by a nice guy in a big house—actually *the* big house. It's a nice gated community, anyway.

Life in the spotlight *does* have its advantages.

Like the time the *Dayton Daily News* featured me on their front page—let me tell you, it opened up some real doors. My friend Pat told me about the call she got from a guy who said I was the perfect woman for him.

"*Really?*" Maybe this was it. Maybe this man was the answer to all my prayers!

"Yeah, Jan. Just wait until you hear about him. He's forty years old, he drives a Harley *(nothing wrong with that!)*, he lives at home with his parents, and he answers to the name...Squirrel."

Squirrel.

Well, what's in a name, really?

Squirrel came to one of my speaking engagements and introduced himself. Nice guy. Shook my hand and simply introduced himself as Squirrel. Just like that. As if it were Bob or Joe or Jim. He didn't try to explain it, maybe mention that he got the nickname when he used to hide nuts as a child or something of the like. No, just "Squirrel." I actually would've been all right if I hadn't had friends standing behind him pretending to be squirrels. Could've done without that.

A Wake-up Call

It's so very easy to get sidetracked. God is looking down at the big picture—wanting to call us into the game. But instead of looking at what He has in store, we're focusing on some guy.

Every now and then we get a glimpse of the bigger picture—the spiritual battle that is beyond our vision and focus. It is more real than what we see, hear, and feel. On April 11, 2000, I was in Evansville, Indiana, where I spoke at a pro-life banquet for 2,200 people. I was signing books after the event when this lady came up and told me she recognized me from "seeing me in a dream." She told me that God had woken her up in the middle of the night—showed her what I looked like and told her to pray for me.

How do you respond to something like that? I said, "Well, had you seen any pictures of me—in the newsletter, perhaps, or in any of the flyers or publicity material?"

"No, Janet. The *only* time I ever saw you was in my dream—I recognized you earlier standing in the restroom, but I didn't want to disturb you." (That would have been moments before my speech, when I was still writing it—I like them fresh.)

She told me, "I'm a prayer warrior."

No kidding.

Now, this lady had no reason to lie to me. She had already paid for her book. And if God is God, the way I see it, He can do whatever He wants. A while later I was in a business meeting with some television production people and one of them, Javier, told me that God had woken him up in the middle of the night, too.

He said he had the strongest feeling—one he couldn't ignore—to pray for protection for me.

I know what you're thinking. Maybe this guy wanted to go out with me and was using this as some kind of inroad. Nope. A more happily married guy I seldom see. My mom has stayed up all night praying for me too. Other people have told me similar things—that they "had to pray for me" because, for some reason, God put me on their hearts. It happened again today.

It doesn't seem believable, does it? That's because you've already forgotten that we're in a spiritual battle. Told you you'd forget. God is real, and prayer changes things. That's why He wants us praying.

Why is God waking people up and having them pray for me? Well, maybe He has something yet for me to do—something Satan doesn't want. That realization helped me to see the bigger picture. It's not about what we see in front of our faces—there is a spiritual battle going on, and we're in the middle of it. But God is more powerful than Satan: "Greater is he that is in you, than he that is in the world" (1 John 4:4, KJV). That verse is hanging on my refrigerator. If we focus on God, He's going to see us through all the distractions, all the hurdles, and all the flaming arrows. Just like a movie. Only real.

This might be a good place to ask for prayer. Will you pray for me? Just think, if you don't, God might wake you up in the middle of the night too!

EVEN THE ROCKS CRY OUT

I was in California at the National Religious Broadcasters Convention. I had a daily radio commentary on 300 radio stations and 250 television stations. Pretty cool. You'd think I would be happy. Instead, I was bawling my eyes out in my hotel room over the guy whose shirt I used to clean my fridge. I was crying out to God to answer me, and I got nothing. Absolutely nothing!

Didn't He *care* how much I was hurting?

The next day I was visiting a church that had Scriptures engraved in the walkway. I was looking down because I didn't want anyone to see that I was crying. Yeah, I went to church, but I didn't get much out of it. I certainly didn't get any answers. As far as I knew, God was ignoring me. Didn't He know what I was going through?

It felt as though He'd never even heard me.

Then I read the verse on the ground right in front of me: "I have heard your prayer and seen your tears" (2 Kings 20:5).

Or...*maybe*...He had.

A lot of people have given up praying because they don't seem to get answers. But God answers *every* prayer. His answers are "Yes," "Wait—I'm getting things ready," or "No—I have something better!" That's the kind of loving Father we have.

Another reason people don't pray is because they don't think it will change anything. That's not what the Bible says. Let's take a look at three times prayer changed God's mind.

Hezekiah: God's 180

If you look at 2 Kings 20, you'll find that God told Hezekiah he was going to die. Isaiah delivered the message at the beginning of the chapter: "In those days Hezekiah became ill and was at the point of death. The prophet Isaiah son of Amoz went to him and said, 'This is what the LORD says: Put your house in order, because *you are going to die; you will not recover*'" (v. 1).

Bummer. "You *are going to die*; you will not recover." Not a lot of room for negotiation. What would you do? You *could* shoot the messenger, but that only helped in the case of false prophets. And if you get a book in the Bible named after you, like Isaiah, I'm pretty sure that you're one of the real ones. God said it. That pretty much makes it a done deal—right? Well, Hezekiah didn't think so; he petitioned God for mercy.

> Hezekiah turned his face to the wall and prayed to the LORD, "Remember, O LORD, how I have walked before you faithfully and with wholehearted devotion and have done what is good in your eyes." And Hezekiah wept bitterly. Before Isaiah had left the middle court, the word of the LORD came to him: "Go back and tell Hezekiah, the leader of my people, 'This is what the LORD, the God of your father David, says: *I have heard your prayer and seen your tears*; I will heal you. On the third day from now you will go up to the temple of the LORD. *I will add fifteen years to your life.*'" (vv. 2–6)

Did you *see* that? God had mercy and changed His mind! *How incredibly cool is that?* Now, Hezekiah could have done a better job with his fifteen-year bonus (see 2 Kings 20–21), but that doesn't change what happened. God heard his prayer and saw his tears and healed him. That's the same God we pray to—did ya know?

The Salvation of Nineveh

Then there was Nineveh. The Ninevites received pretty much the same message as Hezekiah. Jonah, after his aquatic diversion (three nights at the "Motel Whale"), finally obeyed God and proclaimed His message to the people of Nineveh: "Forty more days and Nineveh *will be overturned*" (Jonah 3:4). Again, God said "will be." He didn't say maybe. These people had just over a month, and that was it. How else do you read *"will be* overturned?"

God wanted Jonah to deliver His message, come hell or...high water, so to speak. Listen to what happened next:

The Ninevites believed God. They declared a fast, and all of them, from the greatest to the least, put on sackcloth.

When the news reached the king of Nineveh, he rose from his throne, took off his royal robes, covered himself with sackcloth and sat down in the dust. Then he issued a proclamation in Nineveh:

"By the decree of the king and his nobles:

Do not let any man or beast, herd or flock, taste anything; do not let them eat or drink. But let man and beast be covered with sackcloth. Let everyone call urgently on God. Let them give up their evil ways and their violence. Who knows? God may yet relent and with compassion turn from his fierce anger so that we will not perish."

When God saw what they did and how they turned from their evil ways, he had compassion and did not bring upon them the destruction he had threatened. (Jonah 3:5–10)

Scope it out: God saw how the Ninevites turned from their evil ways and did not destroy them as He said He would. Our prayers reach a compassionate God. And God's mind, it appears, can be changed. If that doesn't make you want to pray, I don't know what will.

Moses and the Whiners

Even the very people who had witnessed God part the Red Sea lost track of who God is. They got tired of waiting for Moses to come down from Mount Sinai, so they melted their jewelry and made a cow to worship. *Brilliant* move.

"Come, make us gods who will go before us. As for this fellow Moses who brought us up out of Egypt, we don't know what has happened to him."

Aaron answered them, "Take off the gold earrings that your wives, your sons and your daughters are wearing, and bring them to me." So all the people took off their earrings and brought them to Aaron. He took what they handed him and made it into an idol cast in the shape of a calf, fashioning it with a tool. Then they said, "These are your gods, O Israel, who brought you up out of Egypt." (Exodus 32:1–4)

Talk about a slap in God's face! He was the one who rescued them from slavery; He parted the Red Sea for these people, led them in a cloud by day and a pillar of fire by night, and dropped their meals down to them from the sky. And how did they show their appreciation? They worshiped a stupid handmade cow to "thank it" for delivering them out of Egypt. God was the one who gave them the jewelry they used to make the cow in the first place—plunder from the Egyptians, remember?

If I were God, I would have wiped them off the face of the earth.

But God didn't. He spared their lives.

How did they thank Him for saving them again? They grumbled and complained: "We're hungry!" "We're tired!" "Are we there yet?" Just like the family road trip. They were sick of eating manna burgers and thought that building bricks in Egypt looked better than what they were going through in the wilderness. I guess the grass is *always* greener—even when it comes to slavery.

We're a lot like the Israelites. How many people do you know who whine about not being married—only to get married and whine about the person they married? Many whine until they get a divorce and then whine about being divorced. If you're the one listening to all that whining, it *has* to get old.

God got sick of it. He told Moses:

> How long will these people treat me with contempt? How long will they refuse to believe in me, in spite of all the miraculous signs I have performed among them? I will strike them down with a plague and destroy them, but I will make you into a nation greater and stronger than they. (Numbers 14:11–12)

But Moses went to bat for the Israelites. He pleaded their case. And that's a pretty tough case to plead—even for a criminal lawyer:

> "If you put these people to death all at one time, the nations who have heard this report about you will say, 'The LORD was not able to bring these people into the land he promised them on oath; so he slaughtered them in the desert.' Now may the Lord's strength be displayed, just as you have declared: 'The LORD is slow to anger, abounding in love and forgiving sin and rebellion. Yet he does not leave the guilty unpunished....' In accordance with your great love, forgive the sin of these people, just as you have pardoned them from the time they left Egypt

until now." The LORD replied, "I have forgiven them, as you asked." (vv. 15–20)

Because of the prayers of Moses, God changed His mind and spared the Israelites. So why did He listen to Moses? "And the LORD said to Moses, 'I will do the very thing you have asked, because I am pleased with you and I know you by name'" (Exodus 33:17).

What terms are you on with God? He *knows your name*, but how well do you *know His?*

You all know the scene at your school cafeteria or favorite campus restaurant. You're sitting eating lunch and people walk past. There are the acquaintances you know from class, but you're not really sure of their names. They get a "Hey! How's it going?" Or "What did you think of that test?" So they know *you know* what class they're from. Then there are those whose names you know, but who generally sit and eat with other people. You say hello and include their name, and maybe even something about them: "I ran into your brother this morning—he says he needs a ride home." But you aren't offended at all that they're eating with another group. They might even ask to eat with you on occasion, when their close buddies aren't around.

Then, there are your best friends—those in your inner circle. They're the ones who rush to your table, throw down their books and coat with a "You're not gonna *believe* what happened!" They never ask—it's a *given* that they're sitting with you. They wouldn't dream of eating anywhere else. Everyone would know something was wrong if they did.

Here's the question: If Jesus came into your favorite pizza shop for lunch, where would *He* sit? Are there people around who know Him better? Would you get a smile and a nod as He found His way to His *real* friends? Maybe a "It was good to see you at Christmas" or "I'm glad everything worked out with that problem you were having."

Or would He come straight to your table. Would you welcome Him, anxious to thank Him for His latest gift, or to seek out His counsel on a decision you have to make?

Jesus would sit at the table with Moses. He was definitely in the inner circle. There are some incredible benefits to knowing God like that: If God is pleased with you and knows you by name, He may do the very thing that *you* ask too.

Prayer has the power to change even the mind of God. Even plans that are already in motion. With Hezekiah, with Nineveh, with Moses, and with you. Think you'll spend more time praying now?

Prayer Changes Things

* And the LORD said to Moses, "I will do the very thing you have asked, because I am pleased with you and I know you by name." (Exodus 33:17)

* I will proclaim the decree of the LORD: He said to me, "You are my Son; today I have become your Father. Ask of me, and I will make the nations your inheritance, the ends of the earth your possession." (Psalm 2:7–8)

* I call on you, O God, for you will answer me; give ear to me and hear my prayer. Show the wonder of your great love, you who save by your right hand those who take refuge in you from their foes. (Psalm 17:6–7)

* O LORD, hear my prayer, listen to my cry for mercy; in your faithfulness and righteousness come to my relief. Do not bring your servant into judgment, for no one living is righteous before you. (Psalm 143:1–2)

* "Therefore I tell you, whatever you ask for in prayer, believe that you have received it, and it will be yours." (Mark 11:24)

* "If you remain in me and my words remain in you, ask whatever you wish, and it will be given you." (John 15:7)

* "Until now you have not asked for anything in my name. Ask and you will receive, and your joy will be complete." (John 16:24)

* The prayer of a righteous man is powerful and effective. (James 5:16)

* This is the confidence we have in approaching God: that if we ask anything according to his will, he hears us. And if we know that he hears us—whatever we ask—we know that we have what we asked of him. (1 John 5:14–15)

GOD IS IN THE LITTLE THINGS

Uh, make that *four times* prayer changed God's mind:

I was on an airplane and lamenting Mr. Wrong in a big way—one of the biggest ways I've ever lamented anyone. Let me tell you how much. Now I'm about as pro-life as they come. But for a moment, when the plane began experiencing turbulence, a thought ran through my mind that was pretty foreign to me. I really didn't care if the plane crashed or not. My life had so fallen apart that I felt I didn't matter all that much.

This isn't a healthy mind-set in general, but especially not for a girl who is traveling to give a speech at the Oregon State Right to Life Conference.

I asked God to get me through what lay ahead, and He did. The plane didn't crash, and the speech went fine. My workshops went well, and the time had come for the long-awaited honorarium. Oh, I'm not talking about money. There's not much money on *this* side of the issue. (The abortionists are charging hundreds of dollars for every child they kill, but we're saving them for *free*.) My honorarium was a day of skiing.

I love to ski. And there's not a lot of it in Florida, at least not downhill. My *one day* of skiing was finally here. My friend Gayle Atteberry, the executive director of Oregon Right to Life, drove while listening to my whining for the three hours it took to reach the slopes. I figure she deserves a mention in my book just for that! Another vanload of people was meeting us there. Yeah, my life seemed lousy and I hated my circumstances, but at least I was going skiing.

We pulled up to the Mount Hood resort, one of my favorite places in the world. You can ski above the clouds, stop halfway down for hot chocolate, and ski to the bottom. As we neared the parking lots, my adrenalin started to kick in. I couldn't *wait* to be on the top of that mountain. But as we pulled into our parking space, it started to rain. Not the kind of drizzle you can ski through. It was *pouring!*

The sky was totally black. We sat in the car and watched as people left the slopes in droves. They weren't just going to the lodge. They were *leaving*—because, as one of the unhappy skiers told us, "The forecast says it's going to rain *all day long.*" Another looked at my hopeful eyes and just shook his head. "It's not going to let up."

And so the crew in the van started joining in one by one. "Yeah, it doesn't look like there's any hope of this clearing up." "Sorry, Janet, I know how much you wanted to ski."

But they *didn't* know how much I wanted to ski! I didn't fly across the country, risk my life in that stupid plane, give speeches I didn't feel like giving, and drive three hours just to turn around. But they had all decided we were leaving. They started packing up their stuff, and even Gayle had her keys in hand, prompting me to head to her car for the long trip back.

"Wait a minute!" It was obvious I couldn't appeal to logic, so they weren't sure what was coming next. "We know the God who controls the weather, right?" They looked at me as though I was a lunatic. You know the look. "Well, He *does.*"

But why in the world would the God who was keeping the

solar system in balance care about something as trivial as this?

Well, He *does*.

I prayed that God would stop the rain so we could ski. I simply asked Him for what I so desperately wanted, and you're not going to believe this, but when we finished—I'm not kidding—the clouds parted, the sun shone through and...it stopped raining. It *really* did. Just like that. If it was a coincidence, it was the best-timed coincidence I ever saw. It was one of the best days of skiing I ever had. We skied *all day long*—without rain. My buddy Philip said he never would have believed it if he hadn't seen it for himself. That was three years ago, and people there are still talking about what God did that day.

He cares about you. He cares about every little detail of your life. He has the hairs on your head numbered, for cryin' out loud. *He is God,* and He hears our prayers. He listens and He answers. And if He controls the rain, then He has the power to stop it. Just ask the people I was with that day in Oregon.

Prayer isn't just for the people in the Bible. It's not just for the big things. It's for us, now, and for every little detail in our lives. Prayer changes things. I've seen it.

MOVING MOUNTAINS

I know what you're thinking. If God really answered my prayer to stop the rain, why didn't He answer my prayer for a husband to ski with?

Good question.

I asked too, of course. If I thought it was a matter of God answering only a finite number of my prayers, I'd quit praying for stuff like weather and pray only about what matters most. I'd hate to waste my "quota" on things like rain. But God is not limited. He is all-powerful. He answers *every single prayer*—in His own time and way.

I just *love* the "Yes, right now" ones! *Definitely* the favorite.

The fact that we haven't yet seen an answer in the husband department isn't an indication of God's weakness. Sometimes it's an indication of our limited vision. He may have the answer just around the corner, but we're not there yet. It may be in front of our faces, but we're too busy looking back to see it. He may have said "not yet" because we're not ready, or because our husband isn't ready. Or He may have something for us to do first. Remember, life really isn't all about us. It's about God. What *He* wants. The good news is that we have a good God who wants to give us "good gifts":

> "Which of you fathers, if your son asks for a fish, will give him a snake instead? Or if he asks for an egg, will give him a scorpion? If you then, though you are evil, know how to give good gifts to your children, how much more will your Father in heaven give the Holy Spirit to those who ask him!" (Luke 11:11–13)

He is *for* us. James said, "Every good and perfect gift is from above, coming down from the Father" (James 1:17). And if our *earthly* father would give us good gifts, how much more will our heavenly Father? Sometimes I remind God that if my dad had the power to give me the man of my dreams, *he* would do it. My dad once loaned me thirty thousand dollars. Said he didn't care if I paid it back. My parents aren't rich, by the way—they took the money from their retirement savings so I could buy the house of my dreams. Maybe your parents helped you pay for college, or helped you buy your first car (as well as feeding and clothing you and keeping you well all those years). My parents wanted me to have what *I* wanted so much that they didn't care what it cost them. That's the kind of thing loving earthly fathers (and mothers) do. (By the way, I finally paid them back—without interest, of course.)

What about my heavenly Father? He *"satisfies [our] desires* with good things" (Psalm 103:5) and "richly *provides us with everything* for our enjoyment" (1 Timothy 6:17). "He who did not spare his own Son, but gave him up for us all—*how will he not also, along with him, graciously give us all things?"* (Romans 8:32).

I can't see any reason why not. Of course, I also can't see much reason why He wouldn't graciously give me all things—including a husband—*right now*. But that doesn't mean He doesn't have a reason. Parents give the kind of sacrificial love that cares about their child's ultimate happiness—for the long term. They want what's best for us—even when that means saying no.

Sometimes we fall into believing Satan's lies. The lies that seem so convincing when we're all alone: "God doesn't care." "He's forgotten you." "Your pain doesn't matter to Him." When we give in to those lies, we let Satan win. God is looking for faith. He honors it.

When the apostles couldn't cast out a demon, they asked Jesus why. And He told them it was because "of *your unbelief*" (Matthew 17:20, NKJV). Faith is an important factor in seeing our prayers answered. "I say to you," Jesus continued, "if you have faith as a mustard seed, you will say to this mountain, 'Move from here to there,' and it will move; and nothing will be impossible for you. However, this kind does not go out except by prayer and fasting" (vv. 20–21, NKJV).

Did you catch that? You *need* to have faith. But if you want the mountain to move, you have to *pray and fast*. How much do you want the mountain to move? I don't have a lot of experience in fasting. Don't really care for it much. But if God said that's one of the components for mountain moving, then I'm going to listen.

One time I really took this seriously was during the 2000 elections.

On the Sunday morning before Election Day, my pastor announced from the pulpit that Christian leaders had called for a day of fasting for the elections and for our country. I had skipped breakfast, so I was a third of the way there. But I came home to a refrigerator full of food—a rare thing for me. I'd just gone shopping and had all my favorite things to choose from. I remember sitting by my pool praying, *Look, God, if that fasting thing has to do with making time to pray, I can pray while I eat! I am fully capable of praying with my mouth full. I mean, I would hate for that food to go to waste. What do You say?*

I didn't get an answer. God didn't seem to respond to what I thought was a very logical case. But it's not about logic. It's not about *our* ways. It's about *His* ways. I understand they're higher than ours.

So I decided to obey God and made it through the day, praying every time I wanted to eat—which was pretty much all day. This election was critical, after all. It would determine who would be appointed to the Supreme Court—who would decide whether we would be able to protect children from abortion in my lifetime. This was everything! If there was ever a time to fast, this was it.

Election Day was Tuesday, just two days away. I thought if I could fast for one day, surely I could go *two more*. I decided that I was going to fast *until I found out the results of the election.*

As you may recall, the results of the election didn't come right away. And neither did food. I fasted for seventeen days—until my family pressured me into eating some Thanksgiving dinner. I went back to fasting after that.

I remember meeting with Dr. Bill Bright of Campus Crusade for Christ one day in Orlando—a spiritual giant who recently went home to be with the Lord. I had skipped lunch, and I thought I was going to die. I was feeling faint and wasn't sure I was going to make it. That was when he told me he was on day thirty-six of his forty-day fast. I left very humbled. I could barely skip lunch without fainting, and yet when I was focused on God and praying for Him to have mercy on us as a nation, I could fast for seventeen days. With God, all things are possible. That includes changing election results and moving mountains. (By the way, here's a secret to fasting: After the third day or so, you don't feel hungry anymore. If your focus is on God, it's not as hard as you might think.)

Have faith. God is God. Pray. He's listening. Fast. Show Him you really mean it. That's how mountains move.

My friend Evan's grandmother was an exceptionally godly lady—very aware of the spiritual battle we're in. She gave me what she said was the most profound prayer she ever learned, based on Ephesians 1 and 2 Corinthians 10:

God, I call upon the power of the blood of Jesus Christ, the resurrected Son of God, to take back any ground I have given to Satan; tear down the strongholds in my life, and build towers of truth that I may see Your will.

Brick by brick, build a fortress that Satan can't penetrate with his flaming arrows of lies. Start with the basics: God is real. His Word is true. He is good. He loves you. Write down everything that you *know* to be true. Then add another layer to your tower: He hears you when you pray. He has a plan for you. He is powerful enough to bring it about. See what I mean? Take back the ground you have given Satan. Build a tower of truth so you can see what God has for you.

If you keep looking at Satan's flaming arrows—at his lies—they can be blinding. They can be overwhelming. They're designed that way. When you feel overwhelmed, pray, *Father I rebuke that thought in the name of Jesus and I plead the blood of Jesus over my mind. I choose to trust your truth over Satan's lies. Guard my mind and thoughts, Lord, in this spiritual battle.* Satan cannot stand up against the name and the blood of Jesus. His weapons will be rendered useless: "No weapon forged against you will prevail" (Isaiah 54:17). Quit focusing on the flaming arrows of Satan and go back to building your tower of truth.

With the shield of faith in one hand—Nehemiah-style—build until your fortress is secure. Just as when Nehemiah was rebuilding the walls of Jerusalem, an enemy is ready to attack:

> From that day on, half of my men did the work, while the other half were equipped with spears, shields, bows and armor. The officers posted themselves behind all the people of Judah who were building the wall. Those who carried materials did their work with one hand and held a weapon in the other. (Nehemiah 4:16–18)

When you are protected by that "tower of truth," those arrows can't touch you. But you still need to watch your back.

Unfortunately—or *fortunately*, as the case may be—God doesn't always answer our prayers right away as He did by stopping the rain that day in Oregon. In fact, I think it's safe to say He *usually* doesn't. That's why we need to be persistent—like the widow in Luke 18. There was a judge who "neither feared God nor cared about men" (v. 2). And there was a widow who kept coming to him for legal protection from her opponent. This judge didn't care about her or her cause, but watch what happened as she kept petitioning him to intervene:

"For some time he refused. But finally he said to himself, 'Even though I don't fear God or care about men, yet because this widow keeps bothering me, I will see that she gets justice, *so that she won't eventually wear me out with her coming!*'" (vv. 4–5)

The judge granted her request just so he wouldn't have to keep hearing from her. How does this relate to God? After all, He *does* care about us. Read on:

"And will not God bring about justice for his chosen ones, who cry out to him day and night? Will he keep putting them off? I tell you, *he will see that they get justice, and quickly*. However, when the Son of Man comes, will he find faith on the earth?" (vv. 7–8)

If a judge who doesn't care about us or our case will grant a request because of persistence, how much more will God respond to us?

In Psalm 37, just after God's Word tells us that, if we delight in Him, He'll give us the desires of our hearts, He says this: "Commit your way to the LORD; trust in him and he will do this: He will make your righteousness shine like the dawn, *the justice of your cause like the noonday sun*" (vv. 5–6).

Just as the widow received justice from the judge, God can make the justice of *our cause* "like the noonday sun." We're only asking for what God said is good, don't forget. And if we're focused on Him, delighting in Him, I believe He will grant our request.

Prayer really works. It changes things. It moves mountains. Have faith, because God is faithful. Trust Him, because He is trustworthy. Focus on the spiritual battle that's more real than what we see, hear, and feel. Call upon the Father who loves you, who didn't spare His own Son for you, and persist until you see Him move. He will. He promised.

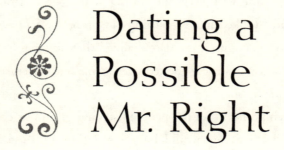 Dating a Possible Mr. Right

WHAT ARE YOU LOOKING FOR?

F ace it. With the right guy, life is a blast. It's like going from a black-and-white, somber world to one filled with color and laughter. You're renting movies again, watching them all cuddled up in front of the fireplace, going out, making dinner together, using up vacation days, walking along the beach. Life becomes magical again, at least when you're with someone completely compatible—as so many men who make it to the boyfriend stage seem to be at first. Life is fun again. No question about it.

There was the guy I took to my brother's wedding. It was an afternoon affair, and I was in the wedding party, wearing a peach tea-length dress with pearls and matching peach shoes. The reception, at the Cleveland Athletic Club, was over by dinner-time. But by then my boyfriend and I were hungry again. So we stopped at McDonald's and went in for a bite.

We stood in line with everyone staring at us—he had on a suit and tie, and I looked like something out of *Bridesmaid* magazine. We got to the counter, my date realized that apparently he was a little short on cash. He looked over at me and sheepishly asked if I had any money.

I looked behind me at all the people listening in on our conversation and decided this would be a good time to see how compatible we really were. It would be fun to make a little scene.

So I slammed my purse down on the counter and said loud enough for everyone in the place to hear, "You tell me you're taking me out to dinner. I get all dressed up and you bring me...*here!* And now you tell me you want to go—*Dutch?!*"

The crowd looked on in horror! My boyfriend played right into it. "Hey, at least I let you drive the moped!" Then he took the lid off his milk shake and held it to his nose to enjoy the "bouquet" before taking a sip, as though it were a fine wine.

We dated for over a year.

Is He or Isn't He?

Here's what happens when you date someone you love being with: That's all you want to do. Working out? No time. Other friends? Forget it. Time with God? He often gets the leftovers.

But if you want God to bless your relationship, you can't let this happen.

Think of a jar that is three-quarters full of rocks and another that is three-quarters full of sand. If you try to put the rocks in with the sand, they won't all fit. But pour the sand into the jar of rocks, and you know what? The sand will fit *around* the rocks. Our time with God needs to be like the rocks. First. First thing in the jar. Nonnegotiable. The sand is the endless list of other things we have to do in life. It can all fit around the rocks. That includes the guy you're seeing.

The Pep Talk

Is the guy you're with encouraging? Is he supportive of what you do? Does he make you want to grow and strive for more? Does he make you want to keep going when you feel like quitting? The best pep talk I ever had was from Matt. I was running for Republican State Central Committee—an office on the ballot during the primary elections—only I was running against the entrenched secretary of the Republican Party. Her son was a powerful lobbyist who raised more money than most candidates running for the House of Representatives. It was an uphill battle—and it wasn't looking good.

Every Saturday for six weeks, fifty people came to my house and from there went door-to-door in the snow so that I could be a pro-life influence inside the Republican Party in Ohio. And every Saturday I bought dozens of doughnuts to feed the troops. One week, instead of taking the usual way home, I thought I would save time by going through the back streets. Trouble is, I'm directionally impaired and I got lost—for about forty minutes. By the time I got home from the doughnut store, I was feeling like a complete idiot. I called my boyfriend Matt in tears.

"How in the world," I moaned, "can I possibly run for State Central Committee when I can't even find my way home from the doughnut store?"

Good question, I thought. *This is going to be tough even for him to answer.*

His response? "Jan, are you running for taxi driver? Are you running for bus driver? Because you wouldn't make a very good one of those. In fact, you'd make a *lousy* cab driver. But that's not what you're running for—is it? *Issss* it?"

That's the kind of encouragement we're supposed to be for each other, able to take the other person from crying to laughing, from disappointment to hopefulness.

A few weeks ago I visited Matt while on a business trip in Phoenix. We went hiking up to the top of Camelback Mountain to see the sunrise. Matt kept making U-turns. I could tell he was lost and was starting to get really frustrated. That's when I gave his *same* pep talk. I was glad I could encourage him in some small way. I told him how that girl who got lost coming back from the doughnut shop *won* that impossible Central Committee seat. And went on to lobby for legislation like the nation's first ban on partial-birth abortion, to influence policy, and to make something with her life...all because of a certain pep talk. Matt got the message, and, while he was pulling me up the mountain, I reminded him that I wasn't running for mountain climber. I was perfectly content to ask the fellow mountain climbers to describe the sunrise—and copy us their pictures—but he made sure we made it to the top.

That's the kind of guy you want.

He's the same one who, when I ran out of Halloween candy, put on my seal mask to trick-or-treat for more. Why do I have a seal mask at my disposal? From my "Save the Baby Humans" entry in the Fourth of July parade, of course. My house is filled with those kinds of props. You can read about all of those adventures in my book *True to Life*. But imagine a grown man dressed normally—except for a rubber, over-the-head, seal mask. Imagine opening your door to this guy saying in a low voice, "Trick or treat." He came back just in time too. I was down to giving out one Andes mint per trick-or-treater.

Well, as I said at the beginning of this book, I'm not the expert on what to do when it comes to finding Mr. Right, but I've figured out a lot of what *not* to do. One thing I've done far too often is make comparisons. When you put together all the best traits of all the guys you've dated, *nobody* is going to be able to live up to that imaginary ideal. Because, for every one of their great traits, those guys you're no longer seeing had some lousy ones too. You know—the reasons why you're not still dating them!

I once dated a guy who would drive five hours just to see me. So when the last boyfriend refused to drive a half hour to see me one evening, I didn't take it so well. By comparison, it seemed he didn't care as much. Not necessarily the case, however—he just showed that he cared in other ways. Some people will write love letters that make your heart melt. Some guys show they care by fixing stuff that's broken around your house. (This is a great trait!) Some send flowers. Some write songs. Others drive long distances. The problem starts when you compare the guy who sends the flowers with the one who fixes leaky faucets. Why doesn't he ever send flowers...? Let the whining begin.

Before you start comparing, take an analysis of what he does do to show affection. Of course, if you can't think of anything, well, then, you may have a point!

I remember when Bob, a guy I dated for two years, sent roses to me at the office. Generally speaking, I think most of us would consider that a pretty good thing to do. Red roses—a wonderful expression of love.

But Bob just happened to send them the same day that Ben, a friend I worked with, also expressed his love to *his* girlfriend...by renting a plane to fly overhead. Timing is everything.

My office overlooked the Ohio Statehouse and we all watched from my windows as Ben was giving Mariely the grand tour below. We then saw them looking up, along with everyone else in downtown Columbus, at the circling plane dragging the words I LOVE YOU MARIELY behind it.

We made some quick signs to hang out of the windows, and clapped and waved as they looked up at us. I relayed all of this to Bob in precise detail, of course, when he called later that day. "Bob, it was like a movie! The plane flew overhead as everyone downtown cheered them on...and, uh, the roses were nice too. *Thanks*."

A few days later Bob walked into my office. Seeing his roses still in full bloom, he asked, "Where's the plane *now?*"

Come to think of it, he may not have rented a plane, but Bob drove six hours round-trip to see me—for two years. Once he drove six hours a day for eleven days in a row. I guess that kind of devotion is better than a plane. When you're doing comparisons, you have to take it all into account. It also helps to date a guy who lives in the same city.

Remember my "little Bobby" stunt at the Grand Canyon? Well, that's the Bob I'm talking about here. When we were flying to Arizona on that trip so I could meet his father, we had a lay-over and walked up to the airline counter to check in. Apparently the flight had been overbooked. We asked if they had seats for us.

That's all we did. I *promise*. But for some reason they got the impression we were newlyweds. We never said that. Never even implied it. We just asked for seats on the plane. But the guy behind the counter made it his mission to find us seats. He declared, "I don't care if we have to *kick people off the plane*—we're going to find seats for you two kids."

The next thing you know, we were being *whisked* away to first class—with people congratulating us all the way there. As they gave us hot towels, the flight attendants asked us how we met. I was trying to tell them we weren't married as they served our filet mignon, but all they wanted to do was comment on how "in love" we looked and how happy they were for us. Then they announced it on the intercom—for everyone on the plane to applaud. By the time they brought out the champagne, we just smiled and hid our left hands so we wouldn't get kicked off. Again, we never said a word about being newlyweds. We might have been holding hands, but they took it from there.

I e-mailed Bob recently to ask if there were any details he would add to this story. His contribution? "Well, you could make it even clearer that I'm the most wonderful man you've ever met." One thing's for sure—I want to be with someone who makes life an adventure.

And how is your guy during the stressful times? My last boyfriend and I were *really* late for a dinner, and it was his fault. On the drive there, I think I reminded him of just how late we were every twenty seconds or so, in an effort to get him to drive faster. I had said "We're really late!" for the tenth time, and before I could tell him again, he said, "How are we doing *on time?*" I think that's when I fell in love with him. It's hard to be mad at someone when you're laughing.

Most important of all, are you "equally yoked"? God is dead serious about this: "Do not be yoked together with unbelievers. For what do righteousness and wickedness have in common? Or what fellowship can light have with darkness?" (2 Corinthians 6:14). A lot of people mess up with this one. Pastors hear it all the time in counseling: "But you don't understand; he treats me so well! He's my soul mate!" That doesn't matter nearly as much as where he is in relation to God.

Assuming you're equally yoked, is this guy a spiritual leader? I want someone I can trust to do it God's way. I'm tired of trying to drag guys along on this path. I'm looking for someone to lead the way. Does he draw you closer to God? If the answer is no, see what changes you can make. If once you make some changes you're still not closer to God, tell your boyfriend. If things don't change, your relationship is in serious trouble. God tells us to "seek *first* his kingdom and his righteousness, and all these things will be given to you as well" (Matthew 6:33). Remember, God represents the rocks—everything else is the sand around them.

But guys are often the focus, and this becomes one colossal waste of time. Think about all the times you didn't make time for your family and for service to God because you were dating some guy—some guy who wasn't the right one, but was someone you invested all kinds of time in...at the expense of everything else. This is another of Satan's tools to keep you distracted.

Keep Your Eye on the Coach

In *True to Life*, I talked about the concept of the "coach." How does the player at first base know when to run? He looks to the coach on third. The coach, keeping track of all that is happening with the game, tells him when to run and when to stay put. All the runner needs to do is focus on the coach and look for his cue. But if he's distracted by the girls waving at him in the stands, or the hecklers, or thinking about the last three times he struck out, or even looking at the scoreboard, he's going to miss the signal.

Our coach is God. He's going to tell us when to run, when to stay, and when to steal...well, maybe He won't tell you when to *steal*, but you get the idea. If we are distracted by the boys waving to us from the stands, or looking at the uneven scoreboard of all our friends who somehow have it better than we do, we're going to miss God's cue. He has a view of the whole game, and He wants us to make it *around* the bases even more than we do. Just getting to first base adds the same to the score as striking out: *nothing*. God wants you to win.

Instead of trying to make Mr. Wrong into something he isn't, quit wasting time. Put your focus back on the coach. Stop fighting with Mr. Wrong instead of making an impact with your life for God.

If you find yourself here, take a big step back. Get a prayer journal, and write down the most important things in your life. Write down what you would like to see God do. Just as there is power in the spoken word, there is great power in the written word. When Habakkuk complained to God about His long silence, the Lord replied, "Write down the revelation and make it plain on tablets so that a herald may run with it. For the revelation awaits an appointed time; it speaks of the end and will not prove false. Though it linger, wait for it; it will certainly come and will not delay" (Habakkuk 2:2–3).

We don't often think of it, but God is sending out angels to prepare our path. That's why prayer is so important—it prepares the way so that all we have to do is walk in the trail that's been blazed for us. The more time you spend praying, the easier your path will be. Pray for what God would have you do; then write it down and "make it plain" so that "a herald may run with it." Then "wait for it," because it "will certainly come" and "not delay."

Write down what's really important. Like the salvation of your family members. Like making a difference with your life. And then having someone to share it with—someone who could help you to accomplish more than you could do on your own, and vice versa. A man after God's own heart that brings you closer to Him. That's what I want. Everything else is a bonus.

Write these things down. And then pray for them. Every day. In fact, start thanking God in advance for what He is going to do.

That's what I'm going to do. I'll let you know what happens.

Obey Him

* "You must serve faithfully and wholeheartedly in the fear of the LORD." (2 Chronicles 19:9)
* The law of the LORD is perfect, reviving the soul. The statutes of the LORD are trustworthy, making wise the simple. (Psalm 19:7)
* "If my people would but listen to me, if Israel would follow my ways, how quickly would I subdue their enemies and turn my hand against their foes!" (Psalm 81:13–14)
* For the LORD God is a sun and shield; the LORD will give grace and glory; no good thing will He withhold from those who walk uprightly. (Psalm 84:11, NKJV)

* Fear God and keep his commandments, for this is the whole duty of man. (Ecclesiastes 12:13)

* "If only you had paid attention to my commands, your peace would have been like a river, your righteousness like the waves of the sea. Your descendants would have been like the sand, your children like its numberless grains; their name would never be cut off nor destroyed from before me." (Isaiah 48:18–19)

* "Therefore go and make disciples of all nations, baptizing them in the name of the Father and of the Son and of the Holy Spirit, and teaching them to obey everything I have commanded you." (Matthew 28:19–20)

Moving Ahead

What Now?

So, what does God want you to do now? Ask Him. Then ask Him to do it through you.

I did. And what did He tell me? Well, I launched a national pro-life campaign—doing something that had never been done before. Just before the twenty-ninth anniversary of *Roe* v. *Wade*—the decision that legalized abortion—we had a pro-life commercial featuring Norma McCorvey, the "Roe" of *Roe v. Wade*; Sandra Cano, the "Doe" of *Doe v. Bolton*, which legalized late-term abortions; and Bernard Nathanson, the cofounder of the National Abortion and Reproductive Rights Action League (NARAL). And guess what? All of these former "poster children" for abortion are now *pro-life!*

The commercial started with the words "You've Been Lied To." McCorvey, Cano, and Nathanson introduced themselves and announced to the viewers that abortion is a lie, that they were once a part of that lie, but they wouldn't be a part of that lie *anymore.* Cool huh? And then the words "Will *You?*" came on the screen as we directed viewers to the phone number and website.

Want to know what's *really* cool about this? I have an uncle who said that what he'd most like to do with his life is win the lottery. When I asked him what he'd do with the money, outside of buying a lot of stuff, he really couldn't say. What would he do with his life if money weren't an issue? He didn't really see his purpose or recognize God's plan for him. Then an amazing thought occurred to me. For years I've said that if I won the lottery (which is hard to do when you don't play), I would spend it on a national pro-life campaign. I'm not kidding. I *didn't have* to win the lottery for God to put me in the place where I was able to fulfill that dream.

My life goal? I'd like to see unborn children protected again in my lifetime. But to do that, we must fill every single vacancy on the U.S. Supreme Court with a pro-life justice. That means that the president must nominate pro-life justices *and* the Senate must confirm them. If we are to win, we also need to unite and take our message to the American people.

As part of this campaign, over thirty groups joined together to send a message to the Senate that couldn't easily be ignored. Along with a note asking for the confirmation of pro-life justices and for children to be protected from all the brutal methods of abortion, something *else* was included in the package: a baby rattle.

Proverbs 31:8 says we are to be a voice for the voiceless—for those appointed to die. If *I* were appointed to die, I'd want someone making a little noise for me. The great thing about these rattles is that when they're unwrapped, they make noise. When anyone touches them, they make noise. And even if they're just thrown away, they make noise.

When we launched this campaign on September 4, 2001, twenty thousand rattles were ready for delivery.

On the morning of the press conference launching the campaign at the National Press Club, I ran to Union Station to get a copy of the *New York Times*. I stood at the box in absolute amazement. Not only were we on the front page; we were *above* the fold! That night CNN ran the commercial on their *Inside Politics* program. I was asked to debate Patricia Ireland, the former president of the National Organization for Women (NOW).

I was also scheduled to be on Fox's *O'Reilly Factor* and on *Hardball* with Chris Matthews—for the week of...you guessed it...September 11. Everything was canceled. We immediately pulled the ads from the air in D.C. and halted all interviews. Here's the amazing thing, though: During that time, twenty thousand more rattles were ordered! That is what gave us enough money to make the ad purchase we'd been planning. As I write this, over forty-five thousand baby rattles have been ordered to shake things up in the Senate!

Don't be intimidated. God wants to use *you*. And He works through ordinary people. That was the case throughout the Bible. Moses? His answer to God was, "Here am I—send Aaron!" David? His own father overlooked him when it came time to anoint a king. Gideon? Kept doing that fleece thing just to make sure.

Think you don't have the ability? As my friend Father Bill Witt once told me, "The only ability you need to serve God is availability." Henry Blackaby points out that God never told people in the Bible to do something they could do on their own. God wants us to do God-sized things. Things we could *never* pull off even if we worked our hardest. God can do more through you in one month than you can do working your entire life without Him.

How? Listen to this:

> I pray also that the eyes of your heart may be enlightened in order that you may know the hope to which he has called you, the riches of his glorious inheritance in the saints, and *his incomparably great power for us who believe. That power is like the working of his mighty strength, which he exerted in Christ when he raised him from the dead.* (Ephesians 1:18–20)

"*Incomparably great power* for us who believe"—that's what is available to us. I used to pray, *God, just show me what to do, and I'll do it.* But it's not what we can do for God. It's what He can do through us. Jesus said that apart from the Father, He could do nothing (John 5:19). If Jesus *Himself* said that, then who do we think *we* are trying to go it alone? "Apart from me [Jesus] you can do *nothing*" (John 15:5). We need to join God in what He's doing around us.[4] "For we are God's workmanship, created in Christ Jesus to do good works, which God prepared in advance for us to do" (Ephesians 2:10).

Forget about your weaknesses and inadequacies. Forget

about your fears. Courage is something we're supposed to *take*. When the apostles saw Jesus walking on the water, they were terrified. Jesus' response to them was, *"Take courage!* It is I. Don't be afraid"* (Mark 6:50).

Trust Him to work through you, and you will see God-sized things happen. Things greater than you can think or imagine.

Be Bold

* "Now go; I will help you speak and will teach you what to say." (Exodus 4:12)
* With your help I can advance against a troop; with my God I can scale a wall. (Psalm 18:29)
* He makes my feet like the feet of a deer; he enables me to stand on the heights. He trains my hands for battle; my arms can bend a bow of bronze. (Psalm 18:33–34)
* There is no wisdom, no insight, no plan that can succeed against the LORD. (Proverbs 21:30)
* "So do not fear, for I am with you; do not be dismayed, for I am your God. I will strengthen you and help you; I will uphold you with my righteous right hand." (Isaiah 41:10)
* "Do not be afraid; keep on speaking, do not be silent. For I am with you...." (Acts 18:9–10)
* No, in all these things we are more than conquerors through him who loved us. (Romans 8:37)

* I can do all things through Christ who strengthens me. (Philippians 4:13, NKJV)
* For God did not give us a spirit of timidity, but a spirit of power, of love and of self-discipline. (2 Timothy 1:7)

WE'RE IN THE SUPER BOWL

Spend time with God. Try to pray for a whole hour without falling asleep. Turn off the radio and pray in the car. Pray while you exercise. Use the waiting time in the grocery line, in elevators, and at red lights to pray. Make it a habit.

So you've prayed about what God would have you do. You've asked for His guidance and looked for His work around you—and still you don't know what to do. Here's what I recommend: Do the good you *do know to do* in the meantime. Too many Christians just pray about things. Don't get me wrong; prayer is critical. But it's just a starting place. In fact, "I'll pray about it" has become sort of a spiritual blow-off. Pray...and then get involved

A friend of mine, former State Representative Ed Kasputis, used to get this all the time when he asked people to help him run for the Statehouse. Although he was one of the strongest pro-life, pro-family leaders there, Christians weren't really interested in making sure he was reelected. They all had excuses about why they couldn't help him go door-to-door: "Can't, church." "Sorry, Bible study." And the dreaded, "I'll pray about it."

His answer? "We're in the Super Bowl here and these people are still doing push-ups!" We go to Bible study and church to see how we're supposed to *live*. Not just to fill our heads with more knowledge. The words in the Bible are there to affect how we live. We're told to be "salt and light" (Matthew 5:13–14) in this dark and decaying world.

Take a look at the great commission:

"Therefore go and make disciples of all nations, baptizing them in the name of the Father and of the Son and of the Holy Spirit, and *teaching them to obey everything I have commanded you.*" (Matthew 28:19–20)

A lot of people don't think it matters what happens in the world around us. That's not what God thinks. We are to witness to people, make disciples, and teach them to obey what God has commanded.

Are we obeying what God has commanded us? Ed Kasputis wanted to be a pro-life voice in the Statehouse, but Christians were too busy to help, too busy reading God's Word to *do* what it says:

Rescue those being led away to death; hold back those staggering toward slaughter. If you say, "But we knew nothing about this," does not he who weighs the heart perceive it? Does not he who guards your life know it? Will he not repay each person according to what he has done?" (Proverbs 24:11–12)

Yeah, you can *say* you didn't know this, but God knows otherwise. This is not a guilt trip, by the way—it's a pep talk! You have filled your mind and heart with the Word of God. Now put it to use!

You were born for such a time as this! You already know that you don't need any special talents. God specializes in using ordinary people. Even the most unlikely people. *Especially* those. So quit making excuses. There aren't any left.

GREENER GRASS

I met Beverly at a speaking engagement in Colorado. She's a lovely woman who told me she was going to pray for me—for that someone God has for me. She sent me the *Experiencing God Study Bible*. She was also praying the same thing for her daughter, who was a single mom.

The next time I talked to her, Beverly told me her daughter had met someone in the lobby of a hotel—and they were getting married. I was happy for her and all, but inside I thought, *How come I don't get to meet a guy in a hotel lobby? I'm in them* all the time.

More than a few times I've wondered why God hasn't done that for me yet. I'm older. I've waited longer. How did all these people get ahead of me in line?

The grass always looks greener. I had no idea that the marriage was a complete disaster. They even suspect that the "knight in shining armor" husband sexually molested Beverly's little grandchild. Charges have been filed and it's a heinous, horrible mess.

How many horrible mistakes has God protected you from?

Perhaps you will never know. It has changed my thinking about how I look at people's marriages. Did you know they're not all happy? Did you know that a *lot of* them aren't?

My friend Cary fell in love and married someone who, it turned out, was just looking for U.S. citizenship. Nice.

I'm glad I was spared that.

Another friend of mine married someone who beat her. I think I'd rather sit at home alone than face that.

My friend Joe caught his wife in the act of adultery...with his best friend—who was also his *accountability* partner. How's that for accountable?

I'd rather wait for someone who is fully committed to God with a track record of obedience. That doesn't mean that Christians don't sin. Look at David and Bathsheba. He really blew it there. God can see us through every kind of situation—but when we don't do things God's way, there's a whole lot of pain. A whole lot.

I sometimes get questions from people who think they'd like to have my job. "How does one go about doing what you do?" "What would I need to do?" They want to be on *20/20* even though it's not nearly as fun as it looks. *Nightline*'s not fun at all.

You know how you get there? You travel the state and speak to four people. Then to ten. Then you drive all day to talk to twenty-four. What I have seen is that if we're faithful with small things, God will trust us with many things.

My reading today was about the talents. You remember the parable. One guy got five. Another two, and another one. The guys with two and five talents put them to work and doubled them. The master said, "Well done, good and faithful servant! You have been faithful with a few things; I will put you in charge of many things. Come and share your master's happiness" (Matthew 25:21). The guy with one talent *buried* his. What was the master's response? "Yeah, you didn't have many talents anyway; it's just as well you didn't use them"? *Not!* Listen to his real response: "You wicked, lazy servant!... Take the talent from him and give it to the one who has the ten talents.... And throw that worthless servant outside, into the darkness, where there will be weeping and gnashing of teeth" (vv. 26–30). *Ouch.*

You may think, *I'm not really that gifted. I can't do what other people can do—so I'll just let them handle it and stay on the sidelines.* But that's really not an option, unless you're into teeth gnashing. Use what God has given you—whether it's ten talents or two...or just one.

What I've seen is that it's a whole lot easier to steer a ship that's moving, or a car that's not stuck in park. It's time to take a step. Get moving, and God can steer you in the direction He wants you to go.

MY BEST BUDDIES...

...Bill and Mark

That doesn't mean that you can't have fun in the meantime. I'm still working on developing those good female relationships, but I have had a lot of really cool guy friends. Like Bill and Mark—

brothers from Cleveland State. Bill and his fraternity friends always hung around my pro-life table. Once, as an undergrad, I was in a formal debate on abortion with a grad student. It was well structured, with questions from the audience. When one of Bill's frat brothers, Russ, was called on, he said, "Oh, I didn't have a question. I just wanted to say that Janet Folger looks very nice today." Everybody needs friends like that.

Once I went to the movies with Bill and Mark, and they thought it would be funny to take my tennis shoes off and throw them. *Really funny*. When the movie was over, *they* walked out, but I couldn't—the floor was too sticky. That's when a really cute usher came in and said, "I'm sorry, but I'm going to have to ask you to leave."

"But they took my shoes!"

"Then it looks like I'm going to have to carry you." He carried me out to the lobby, where another usher was waiting to put on my shoes—like a prince, seeing if they fit me! I gave Bill and Mark the "I won this round" look. They never did it again.

...Matt and Matt

I used to hang out with two Matts: Matt G. and Matt D. It was a *blast*. One of the funnest times of my entire life. "Spell check" on my computer is telling me that "funnest" isn't a word. That's because the people who invented spell check never met the Matts.

Matt G. was an ex-boyfriend and Matt D. turned into a new one. Then Matt G. decided he wanted to be a boyfriend again. It was a *mess*. But before things got ugly, hanging out with them as friends was more fun than I can describe. They used to decorate my house when I came home from trips. Once I came back from Mexico to a "Welcome *a Casa Janita*" theme—*piñata* and all. When I came back from Europe, they had an American theme, complete with flags and apple pie.

Matt D. hated summer. *I love it* and was determined to change his mind. I do that kind of thing on occasion. The three of us did all the cool things to do in summer: drove in the convertible, ate ice cream, drank lemonade swinging in the hammock, went swimming, and bounced on my neighbor's trampoline. We were "summer friends"—summer friends and some-are-not, as the Matts used to say.

...Andy and Mickey

These guys have livened up living in Florida. I *used to* let them house-sit for me. Notice the past tense. One time I came back and my entire house was rearranged. A mattress was in the kitchen with "Fred," a dummy Andy used to drive with in the HOV lane (until he realized the error of his ways), under the blanket with a note to "wake him" when I got back.

Another time, they stuck the magnets that I used on my garage door (remember the Bush-Cheney sign?) to every metal thing in my house. My oven, my refrigerator—with all of my silverware attached, sticking out. And my ceiling—you know the metal part where you can put a ceiling fan? Well, they had pots and pans, cheese graters and blenders, hanging in one room, and a toaster from the ceiling in another. I told you these were powerful magnets. There was also a metal stool stuck to my refrigerator with a stuffed monkey sitting on it.

...and Nick

Nick doesn't really count as a buddy—since I ended up dating him. But before that, we were best friends and hung out all through graduate school. When I called, his father wouldn't put me through to him unless I asked for him in Serbian. Then he would run and even wake him up!

Nick and I knew the phone numbers to the elevators at our university and sometimes amused ourselves by calling people randomly. We would compliment them on what they were wearing, or ask them why they were stopping on the sixteenth floor, for example. Or chat with them on the way down and then meet them at the bottom. Once we called a rather uptight friend in an elevator full of people. A girl answered and I asked for our friend.

"Uh, you're calling an *elevator*," she stammered.

"Yeah, I know. The guy we're looking for is wearing a tan jacket with a plaid scarf...."

I could hear her say, "It's for—*you*."

We chatted for a few moments, as everyone in the crowded elevator stared at our friend—in disbelief that he would get a call in the elevator. When he got out, he said, "Don't you *ever* do that again!"

When Nick called *me* in the elevator, I thought it was fun. I'd act all bothered, and tell those around, "I told them to hold my calls." I would act as though it was an important call, when Nick was just asking if I wanted to order pizza.

I went to dinner with Nick a few years ago in New York—on top of the World Trade Center. We talked about our lives, looking out at fireworks bursting above the Statute of Liberty. It made what happened on September 11 even more real to me.

A Month with God

You've come a long way. You've been shopping; you've had the makeover and gotten back on track with God. You're working out and hanging with your friends and actually laughing again. Now I'm asking you to take a step of faith: Take a month off and give it to God.

It's not so hard—when you consider what God has done for you. Oh, it's going to be hard if you're staring at the clock for thirty days. But I'm asking you to take thirty days and devote them to God. Wake up an hour early to read the Bible. Spend time pondering what your Creator has to say. He's the only One who can do anything about your situation anyway. Pray—and remember to start with thanksgiving. After all, we're told to "enter...His courts with praise" (Psalm 100:4).

Turn off the television and radio and spend time talking to God. Put down the phone and talk to *Him*. Go for a walk with Him—asking Him to guide every step.

Been at arm's length from God? We all have. Imagine, though, if we acted as though we really believed what we *say* we believe. If we were in Christ and His Word was in us—if we were really living it, breathing it, eating it, drinking it, sleeping it. If we really relied on every word He spoke. If we held tight to His promises and listened for His direction. If we looked for His purpose everywhere and in everything.

A few months ago I went to lunch with my friend Sharon. It was around two on a busy afternoon. Normally, with all the work I had to do, I would have just eaten at my desk, but for some reason, I looked up at Sharon and said, "Want to get out of here?"

There was a forty-minute wait for an outside table, and a twenty-minute wait inside. But a man offered us his booth, so we sat down immediately in a section where we'd never eaten before. I told Sharon that I had been learning that God is in the details. So my prayer that day—and month—was for God to control my every thought, my every move, and my every step. "The fact that we're sitting in *this* restaurant, on *this* day, at *this* time is ordered by God."

Sharon nodded, and we bowed our heads to pray over our meal. That's when the server came over and interrupted us. "What are you looking at?"

Now, an easy way to share your faith in a situation like this is to ask your server if you can pray for them. That's what we did. He said a few things before going back to the kitchen. One of his fellow servers came running to our table. "Miss Folger!" she cried. She had heard me speak in her high school chapel years before. As we talked, she told me other Christian servers worked with her.

"Bring them out!" I said.

A young couple came from the kitchen and said in amazement that they couldn't believe that "of all the booths, on all the days," we had sat *there, that day!* For months they had been praying for our server to be saved, and they had just given him a copy of one of my tapes. It was a television show I hosted about evolution, and they said it was "sitting in the front seat of his car right now." Apparently, they thought that now, since he had met me, he might actually watch the tape.

Sharon's jaw scraped the table. God *really* has something to do even with when and where we eat lunch!

If you ask God to blow you away with His perfect plan for you, *He'll do it*. Trust me! Just stay close to Him so that you can hear Him whisper where to turn: "Whether you turn to the right or to the left, your ears will hear a voice behind you, saying, 'This is the way; walk in it'" (Isaiah 30:21).

Just after this lunch I flew to San Diego to speak at a conference and took a few days off to join my Oregon friends for some skiing (this is the same group that was with me when God stopped the rain). They had rented a condo, but the key didn't work. In fact, we had to go back to the office three times—but I was still focused, after that lunch with Sharon, on how God is in even these little things. "If God is ordering our steps, we need to thank Him that we had to go back three times for a key that works—He has some reason for it!"

That's when my friend Gail spoke up. "He *does* order our steps! Let me tell you what happened to me. I have a circular drive-way, and every day for fifteen years I've walked my dog down the right side of it. Every day. Without exception. Then one day—the only day—for no reason, I turned to the left. That "just happened" to be the very same moment that a huge tree came crashing down on the *right side* of my driveway! It would have killed me, my dog, or both of us...had I turned to the right as I've always done."

Whether we turn to the right or left, God really does order our steps. And because we had to go back to get our key three times, I was able to hear that story and pass it along to you. I'm glad the key didn't work. I've learned that this whole experience of life is more purposeful and deliberate than we know. There is a plan, and it's for our good.

Surrender to God, and let Him order your steps.

Get close to Him, and then step out and put together your action plan. Get out a legal pad and make a list of where you see God working around you. In your church. Through Christians in your office. What opportunities has He put in front of you? Examine your heart. Where is your passion?

And *forget* about *that guy* for a minute! What has God put in your heart? What gifts and talents has He given you?

Go to God first and surrender. Surrender whatever or whomever you're hanging onto. Trust Him that He is a loving Father. And, if our own father would give us good things, how much more would our heavenly Father?

THE PEARLS

Did you ever hear the story about the pearls? Well, once again, there was this little girl. She was beautiful, of course—she looked just like you when you were little. This little girl loved the pearls her dad gave her. Wore them 24/7. Wore them to bed, in the bathtub, on the playground. Nothing was going to separate her from her beloved pearls. They weren't real, but she didn't care. Some of the shiny part was starting to wear off, but that didn't matter.

One day, as her father was tucking her into bed, he asked if she would give the pearls back to him. "But, Daddy! You *gave* these pearls to me! And I love them!"

"I know, sweetheart, but I'm asking you to give them back to me. Will you do it?"

Tears filled her eyes. She shook her head. No, that was too much to ask. She couldn't bring herself to part with them.

Every night her father asked her the same question: "Will you give your pearls back to me?"

She couldn't. How could a loving father ask her to surrender her beloved pearls?

Finally, one night when her father asked her, the tearful little girl surrendered. Sadly, painfully, she handed her beloved pearl necklace to her dad.

When she did, he presented her with a velvet box. Inside she found a string of *real* pearls. Glowing pearls. The most beautiful pearls she had ever seen. Her father put them on her, and she knew that she could trust him—no matter what he asked her to do. No matter what he asked her to surrender.

That's how it is with us. Maybe we aren't trusting God enough. Our Father is a loving Father who wants what's best for us, whether it's real pearls, a shiny new bike, or the man He has in mind. "What, then, shall we say in response to this? If God is for us, who can be against us? He who did not spare his own Son, but gave him up for us all—how will he not also, along with him, graciously give us all things?" (Romans 8:31–32).

To what—or to *whom*—are you clinging? What is standing in the way of your loving Father's *best* for you and your life? Surrender to Him fully and look for Him to work.

FINE TUNING

Remember my New Year's prayer? I prayed, and have continued to pray, that God would "blow me away" this year—in every aspect of my life. In my ministry, my family, and my personal life. And, well, He is. I'm launching a new venture, Faith2Action, that will help you put your faith into...action. Thus the name. As I've been saying throughout this book, we love God when we do what He says—when we quit just being hearers of the Word and start *doing*. Faith without action isn't a "nice outlook." It isn't called a "good start."

Faith without action is dead (see James 2:17).

There are hundreds of perfectly good things you could do with your time. And scores of groups you could join. It's all a bit overwhelming. But I don't want good; I want the best. Martin Luther said, "Though we be active in the battle, if we are not fighting where the battle is the hottest, we are traitors to the cause." In other words, you can be the best volunteer in your ladies' auxiliary, but if you aren't impacting the culture where the need is greatest, you're not where you should be.

That's why it helps to have an overview of where God is moving across the country and see where He moves you—to see what the different branches of the cultural war are doing before you choose to enlist. My website, www.F2A.org, sifts through the key pro-life and pro-family organizations and highlights where they are taking the lead on the battles that matter most. I believe those battles begin with sharing our faith—because where people spend eternity matters more than anything else. But we also need to be salt and light in this decaying and dark culture. We need to speak up and stand up before our freedoms are stripped away.

What issues do I feel are the most important? After evangelism, I would list abortion, homosexuality, and pornography as the top three. Why? Well, God hates the shedding of innocent blood and has commanded us to speak for and rescue the innocent (Proverbs 31:8; 24:11). Homosexuality? Why should that matter more than any other sexual sin? Because the homosexual agenda seeks to silence those who disagree. They're teaching it to our children and penalizing businesses, organizations like the Boy Scouts, churches like the Salvation Army, and individuals for speaking in opposition. And pornography? Why are all those children being abducted and molested? Pornography entraps those who view it and feeds those who would prey on women and children. No other issue affects human lives, human freedoms, and the human mind as much as abortion, homosexuality, and pornography.

I'll also be working to link pregnancy centers, state groups, and university students—providing a safe haven where they can communicate and strategize, as well as the tools to get them started. Links will register them to vote and tell them where candidates stand on vital issues.

Speaking of using your time wisely, what about all those romance novels women fill their hours reading? There's even a Christian variety, which I'm sure are much better, but generally, romance novels tend to be unrealistic—setting up expectations of the knight in shining armor that, honestly, I have *yet* to meet. I'd love for this handsome guy to show up outside *my* office on a horse one day. With flowers and chocolate, of course—that goes without saying—followed by a serenade and a private picnic on the beach. That's not too much to ask, *is it?*

Romance novels and soap operas not only waste time; they can actually destroy a good relationship by encouraging unrealistic expectations. I recently heard a sermon from Pastor Bob Coy of Calvary Chapel Fort Lauderdale, on how we break the first commandment by being so caught up in the "goddess of romance." We look to romance to fill our needs, which it never can. "Maybe the next guy will be the knight in shining armor, maybe the *next* guy..." and the pattern continues.

Pastor Coy made a point that hit home—about how women expect the guy to say the "perfect thing." The problem, of course, is that he *doesn't.* We want to write the script for guys, but we can't. Then it would be *our* words, not theirs, and, well, that wouldn't count. Ever feel like this? Ever wish you could hold up cue cards? I have. "Why didn't he say *this?* He could have made it all better!" But because he didn't say the thing we wanted, we're disappointed and the guy is frustrated and confused. It's a vicious cycle I've often been trapped in. You too?

Let's put down the books and the scripts and the cue cards. If you're looking for the perfect scripted response from your man—like the one you just read in that romance novel—you will ultimately be disappointed. Remember, our value and self-worth don't come from what some guy says—or *how* he says it—they come from the only One who *can* satisfy, the only One who will *always* satisfy: the God who made us. And give a guy a chance to say the right thing—not the *thing* you expect him to say. He might surprise you.

I just saw the movie *Kate & Leopold*. And I *liked* it. This duke travels through time and falls in love with Meg Ryan. I left the movie saying, "That's not too much to ask! That someone travel through time to sweep me off my feet. *How come no one ever does that for me?*"

Set your goals and follow through. The fact that I'm writing this book around New Year's has actually helped me a bit. Not only did you get to hear all my New Year's Eve whining, but I had to make the resolution to work on this in the next two weeks. It helps that it's the first week in January. Resolutions are perhaps the toughest to break right now.

Did you ever see the movie *Groundhog Day*? Bill Murray has to relive the same day over and over again until he finally gets it right. Then he wins the heart of Andie MacDowell, whom I met at one of my speaking engagements. Anyway, after wanting to quit trying and even killing himself, Bill Murray decides to use the recurring day for good. He learns how to play the piano, saves lives, helps people out, and wins the girl.

Here's what I'm thinking. I'm sick and tired of doing it wrong too. I want to try it God's way.

I am determined to let God handle this area in my life. I give that burden to Him to carry. I'm going to focus on Him and what He wants to do right now, and I'm going to do a better job of guarding my heart. Kissing may be okay, but *probably not* for hours at a time. I'm not going to fall into the pattern of seeing the person I'm dating every single day—at the expense of God, myself, my job, and all my friends. I'm going to make him do a little more work and plan things for us to do. I'm going to go out with other couples and have more game nights and cookouts—and prayer. I don't want to repeat the same mistakes of falling for the wrong guy again.

Take thirty days and try things God's way. You've tried everything else. Fast. Pray. Ask Him to show you what He can do. That's what I'm asking. And I'm trusting that He is able—not just to show me, but to blow me away. Remember, He can do "immeasurably more than all we ask or imagine."

Don't Be Discouraged

Don't be discouraged, my friend. I *feel* as though we're friends by now. We've been in this coffee shop for days!

It's easy to get discouraged. Remember how my boyfriend bought me a Christmas tree before we broke up? A big, beautiful, live tree from "Big Al"—nicest guy you'd ever want to buy a tree from. Before we looked through every tree on the lot, I took my boyfriend aside and told him that the only way I would let him buy a tree for me was if he promised to help me take it down. I hate taking the tree down. Despise it. Didn't even want a tree if I had to do that by myself.

So he promised.

I looked him in the eyes and said, "I'm serious; don't buy me a tree if you're not going to help me take it down."

He assured me that wasn't a problem.

"Promise?"

"Promise."

So he bought the tree.

It's still up.

If it stays up much longer, I'll need to buy valentine ornaments.

Don't forget that we are in a spiritual war. And discouragement is one of Satan's best debilitating weapons. First he talks you into sinning; then he slams you when you listen!

We're human. We're mistake-making creatures. Most often we learn from trial and error. The reason I'm writing this is because if you can learn from the multitude of mistakes *I've* made, you won't have to make them yourself. The only mistake we really make is when we don't learn. If you—or your friends—see a pattern in your life, listen. It's hard. It's painful. But if you don't listen, it's going to be a lot harder as the cycle repeats and keeps you trapped. I don't know about you, but I don't want to stay where I am now.

Forget about the guy for a minute. What lessons does God

want to teach you? Do you keep breaking up over *the same thing?* Learn from your mistakes—don't beat yourself up, but make an adjustment. This is not about blame; it's about prevention. *"There is now no condemnation for those who are in Christ Jesus"* (Romans 8:1). God wants you to prosper and succeed. That condemnation is coming from somewhere *else*—Satan who hates you. Who are you going to listen to?

Don't let your emotions rule you. Don't let them distort the truth. You are a human being made in the image of God. He thinks so much of you that He had nails driven into His hands just so He could be with you. Think of that next time you look in the mirror. God chose to make you exactly what you are. He loves the way He made you. Unique. Special. Like no one else on this earth. When God thinks of you, He smiles. He's standing there with outstretched arms waiting for you to turn around and run to Him—with your problems, your joys, everything.

Want someone to tell you that it's going to be okay? Want to know that everything is going to work out? That's what *God* does. When you run to Him, you will get the kind of assurance no human being can offer. You can hear that everything is under control—from the One who controls everything. When you take your problems and concerns to God, you're taking them to someone who can do more than listen—you're taking them to the One who can *solve* them.

He can not only help you to know what to do and how to respond (you won't find any better advice), but when you run to God, you are going to the One who can intervene in your situation and *change* the things around you.

YOU ARE REALLY BEAUTIFUL

Once I was dipping my feet in my pool, singing to myself, when I looked up at my reflection in the glass doors. Immediately I thought, *Look how fat I am—yuck!*

What I didn't know was that my boyfriend was watching me. I asked him what he was thinking.

"I was just thinking about how *pretty* you are. You are *really beautiful.*"

A lot of times I have a hard time believing things like that, especially when what I feel is the complete opposite. You know what I mean. But on this particular occasion, I could tell by how he said it that he was *really* thinking it. This time it actually penetrated deep into my heart and erased what *I* saw with what he saw. *He really thinks I'm pretty. He sees the same thing I just did, and he thinks I'm beautiful.*

That's how God is. While we're standing at the mirror hating what we see, He's standing behind us, looking at us and admiring us and smiling. He thinks we're beautiful. And He *is* all-knowing!

Let that penetrate your inner being. Let God's opinion of your value and worth reach your soul. Let it change the way you think about yourself. Let it change the way you talk to yourself when you see your reflection. Refuse to accept what you see even if you're convinced of it. Replace it with what God sees, just like we have to do with our thoughts: Replace the lies with the truth. Regardless of what we feel, regardless of what we see around us, God's perspective is true—and it doesn't depend on current circumstances.

Maybe, like David, you can't see what's around the corner, but you can trust God as David did. You can put your faith in the One who is faithful. Because you know what? We've been putting our faith in people who haven't been faithful. We've been trusting men who haven't been trustworthy. We've gone to them for counsel, and we've not always gotten good advice.

When you feel like running back to the guy you know is wrong for you, *run to God instead.* He's been waiting with open arms to give you everything you're looking for—everything you can't find in another person. The source of your self-esteem. Your value. Your worth. Your comfort. Your safety. He is your listener. Your counselor. The One who can *really* make everything better.

He's waiting. Run to Him.

Okay. Forget my stupid pep talk. Read what God has to say about it.

Be Encouraged

* "Do not be afraid; do not be discouraged." (Deuteronomy 1:21)
* May he give you the desire of your heart and make all your plans succeed. (Psalm 20:4)
* Why are you cast down, O my soul? And why are you disquieted within me? Hope in God; for I shall yet praise Him, the help of my countenance and my God. (Psalm 43:5, NKJV)

* Even youths grow tired and weary, and young men stumble and fall; but those who hope in the LORD will renew their strength. They will soar on wings like eagles; they will run and not grow weary, they will walk and not be faint. (Isaiah 40:30–31)

* "Forget the former things; do not dwell on the past. See, I am doing a new thing! Now it springs up; do you not perceive it? I am making a way in the desert and streams in the wasteland." (Isaiah 43:18–19)

God promises. You've heard that "your future is as bright as the promises of God?" Add three words: "The future is as bright as *your faith in* the promises of God."

IT'S A NEW DAY

God has a mission for you. He has an assignment—a plan of action for you right *now*, and He wants you off of the sidelines and into the game.

But remember, Satan doesn't want that. This spiritual war I've been reminding you about is aimed at keeping you from God's perfect action plan. Satan doesn't play fair—he will hit you when you're down. He is a liar. That's what he does. Consider yourself warned: "Be self-controlled and alert. Your enemy the devil prowls around like a roaring lion looking for someone to devour" (1 Peter 5:8). You are his target because God wants to use you mightily—especially now when you're single and can surrender *fully* to Him to use you in a God-sized way. If you couldn't be used so mightily, Satan wouldn't have to go after you so fiercely.

Waiting is hard. I won't deny it. So get your eyes off the clock and off the phone that isn't ringing, and get into the game. Keep your eyes on the Coach.

Trust that He is a good Father—even when He won't buy you that rusty bike. Give up your crummy pearls so He can provide you with real ones. Get your mind off what you *don't* have and start looking at *Him* and what He has for you. Forget about the quick-fix solutions and let God provide your long-term happiness. Close all the wrong doors. Reclaim your heart from that guy's garage, and give it to God for safekeeping.

Run to Him. He thinks you're beautiful. He has the hairs on your head numbered. He will keep you safe and tell you everything is going to be all right, and then *make sure of it*. He will work it all out for your good, whatever it is. All He wants is for you to trust Him—*now*, while you're in the cave like David, while you're sitting in jail like Joseph, waiting for the stupid cupbearer to remember you. His timing *really is* best, even when we can't see it.

He's the God who can calm the storm and stop the rain. The God who hears the cries of His people—and answers them. The merciful God who can reverse even an ironclad death sentence, as He did with Hezekiah, Nineveh, and the Israelites—or get you reinstated at school, when you deserve to be thrown out!

He is directly involved in our lives—just as He was with Sarah, Rachel and Leah, and Hannah. He rewarded the obedient midwives Shiphrah and Puah with families of their own. He gave

Boaz to Ruth, and David to Abigail. Take your hands off the wheel and ask Him to show you what He will do.

He has made promises, and He'll keep them. *"No good thing* will He withhold from those who walk uprightly" (Psalm 84:11, NKJV). "He *will fulfill the desire* of those who fear Him" (Psalm 145:19, NKJV). "I am still confident of this: *I will see the goodness of the* LORD *in the land of the living"* (Psalm 27:13). David was confident; we can be too.

You must *not* let Satan debilitate you with those lies any more. Trust God despite your circumstances, despite your feelings, and you will be used by Him as you never have been before, in a greater way than you can think or imagine. And yes, when you're not standing around watching the clock, misery will be replaced with enormous productivity. This time in the desert will *at the very least* seem to go more quickly—allowing God's perfect plan for the right someone in your life to unfold more rapidly.

* This is what the LORD says: "Restrain your voice from weeping and your eyes from tears, for your work will be rewarded," declares the LORD. (Jeremiah 31:16)
* So do not throw away your confidence; it will be richly rewarded. You need to persevere so that when you have done the will of God, you will receive what he has promised. (Hebrews 10:35–36)

Count on it.

Now get in the game and persevere so you can receive what He has promised.

FEBRUARY 14

Oh, I guess I should tell you where I am now. As I finish writing this, it's Valentine's Day. Yep—even worse than being alone on New Year's Eve. How are things going for me? Let me summarize: I don't have a date, someone rear-ended my car on the way home, and...my Christmas tree is still up.

Do I still trust God?

Yes.

Is He still in control?

Yes.

Is He still a loving Father?

Yes.

Don't get me wrong; I don't particularly like where I am. But while I'm in this stinkin' cave, I'm going to choose, like David, to trust God. Before God shows us what incredible things He has for us in the next chapter, we have to trust Him while we're in the dark. Remember, trust was made for the darkness.

Oh, and I've had pep talks from my mom, Evan, and Sarah. My mom reminded me about Linda at the beginning of this book. Remember? She had a pretty crummy few months too, and then met her husband. Evan, after telling me about the fun ski trip I missed, told me how God kept the Israelites wandering around as long as they kept complaining. He reminded me of the power of the spoken word and how Satan keeps hitting the buttons that work. And Sarah? She bought me lunch and then called to let me know that she just drove by my ex-boyfriend's place, and in case I was wondering, he was home alone too. Those are the kind of friends you want.

And my ninety-four-year-old friend Greta just called to thank me for all the valentines. I sent her one every day this week—inspired by my mom's Operation Valentine project. It feels good to know that you made someone happy. Counting valentines you send to someone else is *way* better than lamenting all the valentines you didn't get. There *really is* something to this stuff.

Besides, I just broke into the huge box of Godiva chocolates from my publisher. He said if I was going to discuss *What's a Girl to Do?* over chocolate and coffee, then by golly, I needed to have the chocolate. I hate to tell you, after all this time, but I don't really drink coffee—with a name like Folger, you'd think I *would*—but I more than make up for it with chocolate consumption. I just ate half the box in one sitting.

Now I have to go back and reread the section on working out.

I'll just curl up and go over what I wrote about those exercise videos while I polish off the rest of the chocolates. Life is full of simple pleasures.

What's a girl to do?

There you have it.

Notes

1. Beth Moore, *Breaking Free* (Nashville, TN: Broadman and Holman, 2000).

2. You can read about Janet Folger's fight for the right to life in her first book, *True to Life* (Sisters, OR: Loyal, 2000).

3. Dutch Sheets, *How to Pray for Lost Loved Ones* (Ventura, CA: Regal, 2001), 83–4.

4. This principle is more clearly spelled out in Henry Blackaby and Claude V. King's study *Experiencing God* (Nashville, TN: Broadman and Holman, 1998).

About the Author

J anet L. Folger is president and founder of Faith2Action—created to WIN the cultural war by working TOGETHER with the most effective organizations on the side of faith and family. She hosts a daily radio program, *Faith2Action with Janet Folger*, which in addition to airing in many markets can be heard on her website: www.F2A.org.

From 1997–2002, Janet worked as the national director for the Center for Reclaiming America, founded by Dr. D. James Kennedy, where she launched an on-line effort that resulted in one of the largest pro-family grassroots armies in the nation—more than five hundred thousand strong.

Before that, Janet served for nine years as legislative director of Ohio Right to Life, where she successfully lobbied for passage of the nation's first partial-birth abortion ban, which sparked debate in Congress and throughout the country. She also secured passage of the Woman's Right to Know law, parental consent law, fetal homicide law, clinic regulations, and adoption reform, as well as removing all state funding of abortion.

Janet has appeared on NBC's *Today* show, ABC's *World News Tonight*, FOX News, *Nightline*, *20/20*, *Hannity and Colmes*, *Hardball with Chris Matthews*, *Inside Politics*, MSNBC, CNN, *CNN Headline News*, CBS *This Morning*, *Hard Copy*, and *Extra*. Janet has also been profiled in many print sources, including the *New York Times*, *People* magazine, the *Los Angeles Times*, the *Miami Herald*, the *Cleveland Plain Dealer*, the *Dayton Daily News*, the *Akron Beacon Journal*, and the *Philadelphia Inquirer*.

She has debated Planned Parenthood president Gloria Feldt, National Organization of Women (NOW) president Kim Gandy, former NOW president Patricia Ireland, and Jack Kevorkian, as well as spokespeople from the ACLU, the Human Rights Campaign, NARAL, GLSEN, and atheist organizations.

In 2000, Janet authored the book *True to Life*, her life story and the dramatic lessons she learned in the pro-life movement. Her second book, *:30 Seconds to Common Sense*, features a compilation of her award-winning radio and TV commentaries and was published in 2001.

Janet has received an Honorary Doctorate in Christian Humanitarian Service from South Florida Bible College & Theological Seminary. She also graduated with honors from Cleveland State University with a Masters degree in Communication.

Janet speaks all over the country. For speaking engagements, please make all requests in writing to:

Speaking Request for Janet Folger
P.O. Box 633
Dania Beach, FL 33004-0633

She'd also just like to hear from you!

To learn more about Janet and Faith2Action, visit www.F2A.org

or

www.multnomah.net/janetfolger

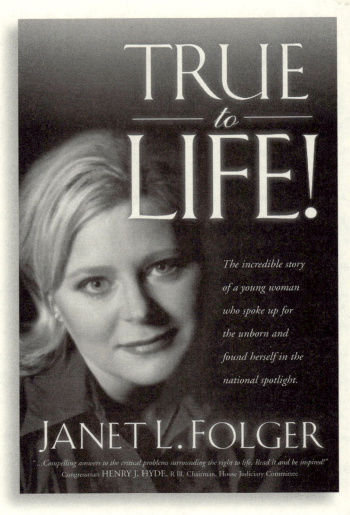

TRUE
— *to* —
LIFE!

The incredible story of a young woman who spoke up for the unborn and found herself in the national spotlight.

JANET L. FOLGER

"*...Compelling answers to the critical problems surrounding the right to life. Read it and be inspired!*"
Congressman HENRY J. HYDE, R Ill. Chairman, House Judiciary Committee

Janet Folger, young, single, and shy, fought for the passage of t[
nation's first ban on the partial-birth abortion—and won!

ISBN 1-929[